The Pond Beyond the Forest

Reflections on Childhood Trauma and Motherhood

Shigeko Ito

SWP
SHE WRITES PRESS

Published in 2025 by
She Writes Press, an imprint of The Stable Book Group

32 Court Street, Suite 2109
Brooklyn, NY 11201
https://shewritespress.com
Library of Congress Control Number: 2025908959
ISBN: 978-1-64742-980-5
eISBN: 978-1-64742-981-2

Interior Designer: Kiran Spees

Printed in the United States

Names and identifying characteristics have been changed to protect the privacy of certain individuals.

To all moms with unhealed childhood trauma

"Until you make the unconscious conscious,
it will direct your life and you will call it fate."

—Carl Jung

Contents

Preface

I was inspired to share my story in part to convey how profoundly my life changed after staying with an American host family in California as a high school summer exchange student. Once I met them, I realized I was being suffocated by my dysfunctional, loveless family and the highly restrictive nature of Japanese society.

The term "complex trauma" does not appear in this memoir, nor do other closely related terms such as "developmental trauma," "attachment trauma," "relational trauma," or "complex PTSD." It was through reflecting on what I'd written that I discovered their definitions seemed to perfectly capture my puzzling symptoms. Neuroscience has shown that prolonged or repeated toxic stress during childhood can alter the developing brain and nervous system, making the child more vulnerable to stress and leading to lasting impacts throughout life.

This, I realized, was what happened to me.

I hope my story brings to life how one middle-aged immigrant woman struggled with motherhood, marriage, and personal happiness while confronting the lasting effects of childhood emotional neglect. And how, by delving into the root causes of her lifelong struggles, she achieved greater self-awareness and acceptance so that healing could take place. Sharing this narrative may serve as an in-depth, longitudinal case study of an "invisible wound," raising awareness about this often-overlooked condition among both mental health professionals and those who suffer from it. I also hope readers with similar struggles will feel less alone and find inspiration as they continue on their own healing journeys.

My host family's lifeline and continuous support are why I'm happily living in the United States today. My fun-loving American host father was particularly enthusiastic about teaching me all kinds of idioms and slang—both useful and not-so-useful, albeit hilarious—and "trained" me to speak and banter in idioms. I've grown to love this colorful element of American English for its playfulness and humor, and "mastering" the vernacular makes me feel deeply immersed in American culture. You will find many of these idioms in my memoir.

Prologue
Fish Dream

I'm five years old and I bring home a goldfish in a plastic bag of water. When I show it to my father and ask where I can put it, he suggests an empty aquarium that's long been sitting in the basement. I go down into the dark basement and release the fish into the tank. But the tank seems too small, and I'm unsatisfied. Even though I wanted to keep the fish, I realize it would be happier in the big pond beyond the forest. So, I scoop it up with my bare hands and embark on the path to the pond. On the way, I accidentally drop the fish, and it flops around in the mud, gasping for air. After a moment of panic, I rescue it and resume the walk to the pond. When I arrive, I release the fish. Though it struggles at first, I'm relieved and heartened when it rights itself and swims away.

Morning Hell

October 2013

I was losing it. Sure, motherhood had been tough all along, but lately, I'd come to freaking hate this job that I had sacrificed both my career and myself for.

It was a school night in late October. I stood in the doorway of my tenth-grade son David's man cave bedroom downstairs. He was still texting, even though he knew the rules: At bedtime, the phone was to be parked in the kitchen. His clothes were draped over the treadmill, and the TV was on even though he wasn't watching it.

I erupted with fury. "How many times do I have to tell you, *go to bed*!" I stormed into his room and tried to grab his phone.

"Leave me alone!" He yanked the phone back from me. "If I'm tired in the morning, it's my problem, not yours." He shooed me out of his room and slammed the door.

My shoulders sagged in defeat. *I'm merely looking out for your best interests*, I wanted to shout but didn't. Ever since he'd returned from summer music camp and our family trip to France, his temper had become explosive.

My husband, Peter, must have heard us because he came down and stood in front of David's closed door.

"Listen to your mother!" he shouted. "Put away your phone and go to sleep."

At first, I was glad he was on board with me for once, but when David didn't respond, Peter threw up his hands. "Can't keep doing this. Gotta get some sleep myself."

As he headed upstairs, I followed him, placing my arm around his waist. "I want you to be more persistent and forceful, so we at least *appear* to be on the same page," I said.

"Ease up on him," he said, entering the bathroom. "Teens have weird circadian rhythms."

"But it's killing me."

For two months, I'd tried everything to help David with his poor time management: turning off the modem at 10:30 p.m., demanding his phone be left in the kitchen, and militantly enforcing his 11:00 p.m. bedtime. I naively thought training him to sleep earlier would help him get up on time in the morning, but all it did was cause tremendous tension between us, especially when I tried to limit his Skype usage with his new girlfriend, whom he'd met at summer music camp.

"Just relax." Peter squeezed toothpaste onto his toothbrush. "Things aren't as bad as you think." He said this casually, without looking at me, and started scrubbing his teeth. When he couldn't even be bothered to interrupt his bedtime routine, it triggered in me that familiar pain of feeling shunned and ignored.

"Don't ever say that again. It's so dismissive." I glared at him. "He's not getting enough sleep and can't get up. You don't understand the hell he puts me through every morning."

I waited for him to respond, but with his teeth brushed and thin lips tightly sealed, he went to bed. I barricaded myself in the bathroom, fuming.

Later, I snuggled on the couch with our Goldendoodle, Biscuit, and sipped a cup of chamomile tea. I should have gone to bed too. Instead, I watched videos of *Saturday Night Live* and baby wallabies on my laptop. The velvety feel of Biscuit's ears, her warm body against mine, and the aroma of chamomile made me sigh. Another Groundhog Day. *What's the point?* The patient, kind mother and wife I'd been when David was younger was gone. I felt like a total failure.

Beaten down, I longed to wake Peter, but he needed his sleep. He was the family breadwinner and worked long hours as a pathologist. I had to prioritize his needs. But these days, I felt increasingly resentful of his carefree nature—the very thing about him that I used to adore. It now struck me more as hands-off parenting and was a major source of friction between us.

What about my needs? I'd been burying them for so long that I couldn't even identify what they were anymore.

I wanted to give David what I received too little of as a child—love, attention, and nurturing. I had willingly sacrificed an academic career for my family and became a stay-at-home mom. In the process, I'd grown numb to my ongoing identity crisis. But whenever I saw my incomplete manuscript moldering in a desk drawer, I felt pangs of shame and regret. A university press had requested it, and what had I done about it? Nothing. My resentment festered, but against who or what? I wasn't sure.

The next morning, I woke up panicked from a nightmare. David had disappeared with my car, just like in the troubled-teen episode I'd seen on *Dr. Phil*. David's friend had emailed me a photo of David driving my car, along with a portrait of me as an ugly ogre with steam blowing out of my ears, both of which he'd posted on Facebook. I was terrified, not only to be demonized like that but also that everyone would find out.

Drenched in sweat, heart pounding, mouth dry, I took a few deep breaths before prying myself out of bed and waddling in my sweat-soaked pajamas to the bathroom. *Whew, thank God it was just a dream.* After sipping some water, I glanced in the mirror. Dark circles ringed my eyes. The skin on my face had lost its elasticity, and the lines between my eyebrows had visibly deepened. Even my hair seemed to have lost its luster. And oh, my stubborn muffin-top midriff wouldn't budge no matter how hard I tried to lose it. Neck and lower back pain made me consume Aleve like candies. People used to tell me I looked ten years younger than my age, but today? Damn, did I ever look and feel fifty-two. I made a lame attempt to pull out a few gray hairs and checked the time.

At 7:10 a.m., I braced myself. *Showtime!* David's fancy digital alarm clock started blasting *Classical KING* at top volume. Nothing woke him up. Like a human snooze alarm, I went into his bedroom at five-minute intervals, nudged him—deep in sleep with his mouth open—and yelled, "Get out of bed!"

After thirty minutes, he finally climbed to his feet, saying, "I'm up, I'm up," his eyes still half-closed as he headed to the bathroom. I crossed my fingers that his shower would be quick so I wouldn't have to drive like a road-rager to get him to school on time.

The saving grace was that we lived close to the school. From the time I was in first grade I had to get up at 6:00 a.m. to catch a train, where I had to stand for an hour and a half on the trip to and from school. I often scurried to the station with a slice of buttered toast in my mouth. The train was so jam-packed I could hardly breathe. If I lifted a foot, I had to remain standing on one leg.

It was one of the many reasons I made sure David had a healthy breakfast: whole-wheat multigrain toast with peanut butter, pan-fried chicken-apple sausage, strawberry Greek yogurt, some fruit, and either milk or chocolate soy milk—all served on a ready-to-go plastic tray. On some days, I enjoyed cooking this feast for him. Today I took one look at the sausage in the fridge and realized I hated this whole maddening routine.

Peter came into the kitchen and frowned at the sizzling sausage. "You cater to him way too much. When I was in elementary school I got myself out of bed and ate breakfast on my own. I even made my own lunch," he said.

His handsome hazel eyes were warm and gentle, but lately they couldn't mask his disappointment at our continual family strife. Or maybe at me? His salt-and-pepper hair seemed noticeably grayer, but I pretended not to notice. I didn't want to feel responsible, even though I sensed that my unhinged behavior of late was contributing to his stress.

Finally, David was ready, and he hopped in the car with his breakfast tray on his lap. I swerved through traffic, glaring at him as he shoveled ketchup-smeared sausage into his mouth.

"Mom, that was close," he said. "You're driving like a maniac."

Although my heart still pounded from a near miss, I banged the steering wheel with one hand. "If we'd left five minutes earlier, I wouldn't have to drive this way."

No response.

"How many times do I have to tell you that you need better time management? I can't go to sleep until you go to sleep because I worry that you may not get enough sleep. And that keeps Dad up, too, and then he gets mad at me for keeping him up."

Why can't he see that he's the problem here? The trouble was that David's textbook adolescent behavior—sleep issues, crankiness, mood swings, emotional volatility—was almost identical to my menopausal symptoms. On good days, I could keep my temper in check. But more often than not, our interactions turned into an adolescent versus menopausal Battle Royale.

He took a bite of his toast and turned to me. "You know, Mom, the issues you're dealing with have nothing to do with me and Liz." He was enraptured by that girl. "Liz and I have just exposed the issues you and Dad already had," he said, while he continued to chew. "You should stop online shopping. That's upsetting Dad more than my Skyping. You and Dad should see a marriage counselor."

I couldn't look at him. I often hid the purchases in my closet, only to return them later when I was overcome by regret and guilt . . . which made me the Queen of Returns. Peter called me a retailer's nightmare. But I couldn't stop.

The smirk on David's face made me want to smack him. He thought he had it all figured out; he was the smart one in the family, and his parents knew nothing because we were stupid, ignorant, clueless, out of touch, or all of the above.

But did I keep my mouth shut? Of course not. I took the bait.

"Dad and I are doing just fine. Thanks for your concern, Dr. Phil." The sweat beading up on my forehead announced the start of a hot flash. "You're a major source of our problems," I shouted. "You're driving a wedge between us." I felt a wave of resentment, feeling that despite everything I was trying to do for him—always at his beck and call—he was disrespectful and ungrateful. Sure, he was a teenager, but this was too much.

"That's a good one; let me record that." He whipped out his phone and started typing. "Okay, today Mom said, 'You're driving a wedge between us.' Anything else you want to add?"

"What the hell are you doing?"

"I'm recording your comments in case I want to share them with my friends," he sneered.

It was my nightmare come to life. "You've got to be kidding. You can't reveal what's going on in your family." I imagined how it would spread at school. I'd grown up in Japan; in my family, public image was everything. I couldn't shake this feeling, even after living in America for thirty years.

I was almost in tears, the back of my shirt drenched with sweat. "If you keep this up, I'll take away your Skyping privileges."

Liz. She worried me. Her soft, delicate voice, the twinge of sadness in her eyes when she smiled. She reminded me of myself as a teen. It was a terribly frightening thought.

David opened his door as though he was about to jump out of the moving car.

"David, don't do that!" My heart pounded with the image of him getting seriously hurt.

He closed his door, seeming pleased to have gotten the reaction he wanted.

"It's so dangerous," I said. "Calm down. We're almost there."

When we got to school, he slid the breakfast tray onto the floor, grabbed his bag, and, without a word, got out of the car and slammed the door.

I drove home in a daze. Ever since the academic year had started, weekday mornings had been rough, but we'd never lashed out at each other like this. Warning bells went off in my head, even though I knew Peter would downplay it. He'd call David's behavior typical and mine an overreaction, but lately I'd grown skeptical of his judgment.

During a recent wellness visit, David's pediatrician had said to me, "Let him fail."

I couldn't imagine following that advice either. Still, something had to change. But what and how? Family counseling crossed my mind. But just the thought of hunting for a good therapist intimidated me.

This feeling of being at a loss reminded me of my early motherhood years when I'd been so exhausted, overwhelmed, and totally alone, not knowing where to turn for help. Except that now I had friends. I just didn't want to burden them with my frustrations and complaints.

My mind flashed back to a glorious autumn day when David must have been three years old. We'd wandered around the Woodland Park Zoo together, and as we visited the giraffes, he gave me a gleeful little-boy smile, wearing his favorite Paddington Bear coat and stuffing his hands into the pockets. *Where has my sweet boy gone? What's gotten into him? Or into me, for that matter?*

I knew emotions were contagious, and my losing it certainly wasn't helping. But that morning I realized something terrible: I had no control over myself anymore.

Barabara Family

Circa 1960s to early 1980s

When I was growing up in Japan, family friends often used the mimetic word *barabara* to describe my family. It means separate, scattered, broken up, torn, or ripped apart, depending on the context. It's generally used to describe a state of separation and disconnection, but it can also refer to the dismemberment of a human body, as in a *barabara* murder case.

I grew up not knowing much about my father, mother, and two brothers. They were hardly ever around, and we rarely communicated with each other, let alone ate meals together. We were like strangers who happened to share the same house, living separately in different spheres—an unusual arrangement in a culture that prizes close-knit families. In ours, family activities were minimal, except for a few occasions. There was the beach vacation we took when I was in third grade, and on some Sundays when my father was free, we dined out at a nearby restaurant above a car wash. Both my brothers joined in these Sunday outings, and we all dressed up as if we were going to church. While Dad's beloved Jaguar was being washed downstairs, we ate corn potage with crispy, buttery croutons and juicy muskmelon dessert, using our best table manners. I relished every moment of our time together and wished it would happen more often.

My father was a tireless surgeon who founded his own hundred-bed hospital with over 120 employees, right across the street from where we lived. The hospital provided outpatient, inpatient, and emergency room services. Once a month (sometimes bimonthly), he was responsible for most of the nighttime ER care in the area. Every time I heard the loud *wee-ooo wee-ooo* of the ambulances, my heart jumped, but Dad was happy as it meant more opportunities to fill inpatient beds. "Working like a *bashauma*" (a carriage horse) was his favorite phrase to describe his work ethic. While I respected his seemingly bottomless stamina and was always amazed by it, even as a child I was concerned about the toll his lack of sleep and excessive adrenaline might take on his health.

I rarely saw him, as he split his time between the hospital and community engagements, such as the Rotary Club and Boy Scouts. But I knew he loved and cared about me deeply in his own way.

"*Me ni iretemo itakunai*," he would say. "You are so dear to me that even if I put you in my eye, it wouldn't hurt." It was a term of endearment very similar to the phrase "apple of my eye" in English. He often showed his affection by giving me big hugs and kissing me on the cheek.

My mother didn't work, but she had an extremely busy social life. Later on, she became heavily involved in the Girl Scouts and Soroptimists (a women's high-society version of the Rotary Club), but when I was little, she was out every day with her socialite friends. One of them owned a bowling alley, and Mom spent hours each day bowling with them. They dressed like professional bowlers in colorful bowling outfits with matching shoes and bags to carry their monogrammed bowling balls. She became quite adept at the game, participated in tournaments, and brought home many trophies. When she wasn't bowling, she shopped, dined out, or partied with her friends until late at night.

Once when I developed a very high fever and started to hallucinate, Mom showed genuine concern for me. I might have been five or six. While she held me on her lap, the moss-green duvet undulated before my eyes like waves. "Look, Mom," I shouted, pointing toward the ceiling, "there goes Mighty Mouse!" Tears fell down her cheeks. "Why are you crying, Mama?" I asked, and she hugged me without saying a word. Days after I recovered, I overheard her say to someone, "When she asked me why I was crying, I knew she wasn't too far gone."

I had two older brothers, Jun-chan and Hiro-chan, respectively five and eight years older than me, but I hardly knew them as they were usually out doing their own things. I've always liked and respected Hiro-chan. He was stoic and didn't say much, but he was kind to me and gave me a nice leather pencil case when I was accepted into middle school and a classy Parker ballpoint pen upon my high school graduation. Jun-chan, on the other hand, was a bully.

"You're fat. You better lose weight," he'd say to me in front of his gorgeous girlfriends, or, "Why do you always look like such a little kid?"

I'd stick out my tongue and pretend to ignore him, but his comments stung.

My father was very strict with Jun-chan. Once, Jun-chan chased me around the house with a small King Tut mask that terrified me. When I cried, Dad, infuriated, chased him until Jun-chan trapped himself behind a table. Dad shoved the table into his chest, and Jun-chan yelped. I sometimes wondered if Mom's overprotectiveness toward Jun-chan might have dated back to those early years.

Hiro-chan (then a medical student) was still living with us when

I was in middle school, but I didn't see him much as he was either out or stayed in his room. He rarely interacted directly with Mom. One night, I came upon a note that looked like it had been written angrily and hastily. It read, "I need 50,000 yen (approximately 250 USD) by tomorrow for my war chest." Mom then left the money on the table the next morning. This was his typical method of communication with her whenever he needed money. He was a heavy smoker and quick to anger, and his outbursts were usually directed at Mom.

"It's like walking on eggshells around him," I often overheard her say. She was afraid of him. One day he shouted at her for coming home late.

"If you keep that up, something bad will happen to Chako." (Chako was my nickname.) He stormed upstairs to his room and slammed the door. That was the moment I realized he cared about me. When I shared this incident with his then-girlfriend (now wife) Kyoko-san, she told me he'd long been concerned about me.

I had a revolving cast of surrogate caregivers, many who worked at my father's hospital. Even as a little child, I was an expert in *tanuki neiri*—"raccoon dog sleeping" or pretend sleeping. As the caregivers tiptoed out of my bedroom to go home, I'd open my eyes and start crying so they'd have to stay with me longer.

I was fortunate to have Yamada-san, a dedicated hospital business office worker, who provided some continuity in my care from infancy through primary school. She would carry me on her back in an *onbuhimo* (a traditional Japanese-style baby carrier) while she worked, then take me to her home overnight and bring me back the next morning. Her two daughters were much older than me but treated me like their little sister. When I developed jaundice, Yamada-san took me to the doctor. After each appointment, she took me to a toy store and bought me outfits and accessories to go with my felt dolls.

I liked Yamada-san and her family very much and enjoyed spending time with them. But by the time I reached middle school, I was old enough to be left alone, and she'd retired. After that, we rarely saw each other. When I occasionally ran into her on the way back from school, we were so happy to see each other. With tears in her eyes, she'd ask how I was doing, which made me tear up too.

I did not like the house I grew up in. Sure, it was built with fine craftsmanship and high-quality woods. There was a beautiful indoor rock garden lit up by an old-fashioned Japanese lantern with zillions of tiny white pebbles around its base. But the lack of windows made it gloomy.

And it was cluttered. There were piles of stuff everywhere, in every room, lining every hallway and the stairs. Every drawer in the house was jam-packed and difficult to open. Japan is a gift-giving culture, and we received many presents from my father's patients' families, especially during the two traditional gift-giving seasons in summer and winter. There were beautifully wrapped soaps, premium cooking oils, beer, and gourmet muskmelons nestled in attractive wooden boxes. But many of the boxes stayed unopened for months. Fancy oranges rotted before we had a chance to eat them. The rest of the gift boxes ended up stored away in two sheds outside our house.

It wasn't my father's patients or their families who were the problem. The major cause of this chaos was my mom, whose passion was shopping. Two rooms in our house had been turned into storage, mostly for her purchases. Once, I inadvertently opened the door to one of the rooms, looking for some loose coins in Mom's handbag, without realizing my tutor was behind me.

"Wow!" she gasped. "What's up with that room?"

Embarrassed, I slid the door shut. "Umm, it used to be Mom's room, but it's now a storage room." I had no idea what might have been in the mountains of stuff that had been collecting dust for years.

The other storage room was even more disturbing. The only space available was at the front, just enough to store a small canister vacuum cleaner. The rest was taken up by box after box of unknown things piled nearly to the ceiling. The room had translucent *shoji*-screen sliding doors, and when I turned on the hallway light, I could see the shadowy silhouettes of a wardrobe cabinet, dresser, and mirror (the scariest of all). It terrified me to walk past this room, especially at night.

My deep-rooted fear of the world didn't only come from those suffocating spooky rooms but also from Mom's superstitious beliefs. She had a phobic reaction to anything that reminded her of Buddhist death rituals. Sticking chopsticks upright in a bowl of rice, wearing clothes inside out, and *kita makura* (a north-facing pillow because of how corpses are positioned at Buddhist funerals)—all of these things terrified her.

"If you cut your nails at night," she warned me many times, "you won't get to say goodbye to your parents on their deathbeds."

I feared the numbers four (death) and nine (suffering), and never *ever* slept with my belly exposed during a thunderstorm. Why? Because of the thunder ogre, of course. It would snatch my belly button!

As a child, I learned to cope with loneliness and stress by seeking comfort from animals, including dogs, koi, and tadpoles my grandmother gave me. I especially enjoyed raising baby birds and feeding them millet (soaked in water overnight) using the tip of a chopstick. They grew attached to me and liked to be stroked or sit on my shoulder.

One day when I was in first or second grade, while playing with my very first bird, Pii-chan, I fell asleep on the tatami floor. I woke up and found her squashed beneath my back. I was grief-stricken and cried uncontrollably. The same thing happened to my second bird, Chii-chan.

When Mom saw me sobbing and holding the lifeless bird, she said, "If you keep killing animals like that, they'll come back and haunt you as ghosts." I was already afraid of darkness and ghosts. That night I cried myself to sleep.

Still, Mom and I shared one enjoyment: monthly shopping trips to Shinjuku Isetan, a high-end department store in the central district of Tokyo. One Sunday when I was ten years old we got up early to maximize the store's open hours. Mom took extra time to apply makeup and put on a floral-print Leonard dress, Ferragamo heels, and a sapphire necklace with matching earrings. I wore an elegant velvety dress, black enamel Mary Janes with lacy, frilly ankle socks, and a floral headband. We took a taxi to Machida Station and bought round-trip tickets for the Romancecar, a luxurious, nonstop express train with seat assignments, to get to and from Shinjuku Station.

I loved riding this train; the seats were so comfortable. On the forty-five-minute ride, we ate ham-and-egg salad sandwiches and drank iced tea we'd bought from a cart full of tasty snacks and drinks.

Once we got to the department store, Mom spent at least an hour in the shoe section. I waited patiently on a leather ottoman facing a fragrance counter and observed well-dressed women sampling different perfumes. Mom then took me to the children's clothing department, where they sold the brand Child. She liked Child clothes for their classy designs and muted colors. While I tried out several outfits handpicked by our usual sales representative, Mom disappeared. I was terrified she might have left me. The saleswoman reassured me and helped me find her. Mom had drifted over to the women's clothing department, completely oblivious to the fact that she'd forgotten me. Mom was easily distracted.

When it was time for lunch, we went to the top floor and chose an Italian restaurant. We ordered spaghetti Bolognese. I enjoyed every bite. (I had developed a penchant for Italian cuisine as I sort of grew up on it, frequently ordering takeout from a neighborhood Italian restaurant.) In the midafternoon, we went to a coffee shop and had cheesecake with tea. This little break helped fortify us for the final hour or two of shopping before the long trip home. The day was a great reprieve from the drudgery of my usual routine.

The house was a place of darkness and emotional heaviness. When I was around eight, Dad found out Mom was having an affair with her bowling instructor and threatened to divorce her. The argument went on for days. I still remember one scene with a bunch of adults—many of them my father's employees, along with some family friends—gathered at our house. One of them was the chief business administrator, Mr. Tamura, who'd always been at my parents' side and was intimately involved in our family affairs. The atmosphere was somber and gloomy. The adults sat in the living room around my parents and stared at the tatami floor as they weighed in on whether my parents should divorce. We didn't seem to have any relatives, or so I thought back then, but unlike most Japanese who prefer keeping things private, it was typical of my parents to involve others in making big decisions. During this period, I was afraid to come home. After getting off at the bus stop, my steps would get heavier and heavier as I approached our house.

One day when I returned from school, all of the curtains were closed and the lights were off. I found Mom sitting with clenched fists at the coffee table. There was a bleeding bite mark across one of her eyelids. When I asked her what happened, she said, "Dad bit me," and started to sob.

When Dad came back from the hospital, the fight continued. I'd never seen him so violent before, and I was terrified. When he was about to hit her, I stood in front of her to protect her. He shoved me aside so hard I fell to the floor. I cried and rushed outside. I ran through the neighborhood thinking, *Dad's turning into a monster! It's a madhouse. There's nothing here for me.* After running around the block several times, I became exhausted and went home, hoping their fight was over.

That night, Mom cried as she lay down on her bed. I tried to comfort her by hugging her and rubbing her back. I wished someone would comfort me. But I didn't think of reaching out to anyone—and who would I have reached out to? I had to be strong for Mom and weather the storm with her. I lay next to her and continued rubbing her back as the Yokohama Line train passed thirty feet away, shaking the house.

Music Camp

July 21, 2013 to August 4, 2013

"Mom, I hate this," David said during a call home from summer camp. "It's like a cram school. We have to practice all day long except when we sleep or eat."

"Wow, that sounds really tough." I'd hated cram school too. I had been forced to attend after-school and weekend-accelerated classes designed to prepare students for the entrance exams to prestigious colleges. It was such a soul-crushing experience. I'd felt like a total failure because I couldn't keep up.

Many of the students at David's music camp were from the Seattle Youth Symphony Orchestra (SYSO). Others had been through the program before and knew the routine. He was discouraged, intimidated, and overwhelmed, and he worried he didn't belong there. I felt his pain intensely but tried to stay calm and upbeat.

"You've just started. Give it some time, and you'll get used to it," I said, pretending to be unrattled. But after I hung up, I paced the kitchen trying to calm myself down. His competitive nature didn't help, nor did his tendency to take things personally. He was being extra hard on himself—something I knew well. I sometimes wondered if I'd passed this trait on to him.

That evening, Peter reminded me of David's tendency to exaggerate and be melodramatic. So, when David called on the third day, particularly frustrated over his lack of progress, I was better prepared.

A kid at camp had been sent home because he'd developed tendonitis. "I hope I get it too," David said, "so I can go home."

Instead of panicking and fanning the flames (my mother's preferred strategy when dealing with me), I just let him blow off steam.

"It's only been a few days," I told him. "Hang in there a little while longer, and maybe you'll get used to the routine." I reminded him he was there for the experience and didn't have to work himself into the ground. "If it's still too much, you can come home. Let's talk again tomorrow, okay?"

After hanging up the phone I couldn't relax. I was worried I'd set him up for failure. My heart pounded so fast I became lightheaded. It never occurred to me to question whether feeling his emotions like this was normal and healthy.

The next day, I called the camp office to ask how David was holding up.

"He seems to be doing quite well," the representative said. "And he's such a sweetheart."

"Really?" I told her that David had been telling me how hard it was for him. "Is it typical for a newcomer to get so overwhelmed?"

She assured me it was quite common because of the intense practice schedule. "They get used to it."

Her words briefly gave me peace of mind. But even so, in addition to sending him a big care package full of his favorite snacks, I called him every evening to see how he was managing. No matter how often Peter reminded me that David needed to deal with the discomfort on his own, I was consumed by the idea of him being beaten down. I needed those nightly calls to calm *my* anxiety.

But my worries were unwarranted. David sounded more optimistic with each day. Toward the end of the first week, he said, "Mom, I'm making good progress." He'd moved up from the thirteenth chair to the fourth in the first violin section. "Unless I really screw up, that will be my place for the rest of camp," he chuckled, clearly confident he wouldn't mess up.

I exhaled a deep sigh of relief.

During the second week of music camp, David transformed into a totally different person—lighthearted and more confident.

"I met a girl named Liz who plays cello," he told me one evening. "I've been hanging out with her and her friends."

Despite my earlier worry over how hard he'd been practicing, I now leapt to the other extreme. "Are you practicing enough to keep up with the others in the camp?"

"Yes, yes." Finding Liz had made him seem more carefree, and he was no longer working himself as hard as he had during the first week. And more importantly, he no longer felt isolated and lonely.

David's sixteenth birthday fell on Friday, two days before the end of camp. Peter came up with the fantastic idea of getting a local bakery to deliver a birthday cake so the other two hundred students could help David celebrate.

Peter comes from a tight-knit family who really values each other's birthdays. His mother hasn't once forgotten to send me a birthday card since Peter and I got married.

We ordered two large sheet cakes, enough for all the students to have a piece, and arranged to have them delivered. We had the bakery decorate one cake with a piano drawing and the message "Happy Birthday, David," and the other with a violin and the message,

"Congratulations Marrowstone students for your musical achievements." We thought they all deserved a pat on the back. We could hardly wait to hear David's reaction.

By the time the students got their cake, however, it had been cut up into small pieces, so they never got to see the decorations. What a letdown. Thank goodness one of the program coordinators emailed us a "before" photograph. David was touched by our thoughtful gesture, and in the end that should have been all that mattered. But I had a hard time letting go of the grievance and stewed about it all night.

On Sunday, the last day of music camp, we drove ninety miles north to Bellingham to attend the final performance at the concert hall and bring David home. As soon as we were seated, we looked for him onstage. There he was, proudly seated in the fourth chair, first violin. He played with passion, enthusiasm, and confidence.

"He's doing great," I whispered to Peter, and he nodded. We smiled at each other and held hands.

During the performance by the higher-level group, I studied each girl in the cello section, wondering which one might be Liz. David often had a girlfriend or two, but none of them had ever been serious. I expected this time around would be short-lived too.

After the concert, Peter and I waited in the car for David to come out of the concert hall. It was midafternoon, a beautiful, sunny, late-summer day, and the university campus was lush with shrubs and flowers. Students and their families poured out of the building and milled around outside, enjoying the perfect weather, while we watched and waited . . . and waited.

David was taking so long that Peter decided to go check on him. While he was gone I fumed some more about the sheet cake.

After fifteen minutes Peter returned—without David, but grinning. "I met her."

"What does she look like?" I asked. *Why isn't David here?*

"She's cute. David's still talking with her. He seems very reluctant to leave."

We waited for several more minutes, growing increasingly impatient, until Peter finally said, "You go check."

I got out of the car, navigating the labyrinth of students and parents in the outdoor pavilion. Finally, I found David talking with a girl with light-brown, wavy hair that fell to the middle of her back. She had an ethereal appeal, like an angel, and looked more mature than David.

"Hey, David. Time to go!" I shouted, waving my hand.

He glanced at me, dismayed, then turned back to the girl and continued talking. I felt dismissed and a bit offended, but I didn't want to make a scene.

Liz—it had to be Liz from the intimate way he leaned toward her—was about the same height as David, very feminine, with porcelain skin and delicate features. Her big hazel eyes seemed unfocused and dreamy as she glanced at me.

I waited several feet away for David to introduce me, but he didn't. I was a little taken aback but tried not to take it personally. Passive by nature, I tended to tolerate such rudeness rather than stand up for myself.

When he finally parted from her, I heard him say, "I love you." It seemed a bit intense for someone he'd just met, but I kept mum. He was a teenager.

The crowd had thinned, and I was able to admire the green lawns and carefully landscaped gardens.

"That girl you were talking to, was that Liz?" I asked as we made our way to the car.

"Yep. She's a member of SYSO." He sounded awestruck.

"That's impressive," I said, and meant it. "Why didn't you introduce me?"

"I didn't feel like it." After a grudging glance at me, he looked back at her, clearly hoping that would be the end of it.

But I wanted him to open up more. "She's really cute, and a good cellist, too, right?"

"Yeah, she's very good," he said.

"Has she been playing cello for a long time?"

During the concert intermission, I'd talked to a twenty-two-year-old woman who'd been playing violin since she was two years old. When David was two, all we wanted to do was get him to sleep. Focusing on achievement while he was still so young was something I detested. Yet, now I worried I might not have been pushing David enough.

All his life, it had been my nagging internal struggle: I wanted him to be happy but also successful. I encouraged him to develop his own motivation in subtle and maybe stealthy ways. For instance, I seldom acknowledged his achievements. Although this might have had something to do with growing up in the Japanese culture of humility, my tendency to trivialize achievements had been doubly reinforced by my family. They rarely paid attention to anything I did.

As David and I reached the car, I tried to engage him in conversation, but he wasn't in a talkative mood. I told myself he must be exhausted after the intense music camp, but it was hard to reconcile that with how animated he'd looked while talking to Liz.

He remained silent for the first twenty miles back to Seattle. I pretended not to be bothered by it and instead admired the ocean views and lush evergreens along the highway.

Finally, I couldn't take it anymore. "Is something bothering you?"

"I miss Liz."

Peter and I looked at each other and rolled our eyes. *There he goes again, Mr. Drama King.* I often wondered if his artistic streak was to blame for his tendency to become so intense and melodramatic, not to mention his high sensitivity. But then I remembered how miserable I'd felt at age sixteen when I had said goodbye to my American host family in California after a summer homestay program. It pained me to think he might be equally depressed about returning home with us.

"What did you think of the concert?" David asked.

"It sounded very good," Peter said.

"Is that *all?*" David's voice got louder. "How did you think I was doing?"

"You looked like you were playing well," Peter said. "I couldn't hear your violin per se, so I can't tell how well *you* played. But you looked good."

"I just *looked* good?"

Oh my goodness.

"What else do you want me to say?" Peter already sounded annoyed, probably because of how long we'd had to wait for David after the concert. "Are you fishing for compliments?"

This was a classic standoff between David's passionate nature and Peter's rational disposition. Peter is stoic, embodying the virtues of the humble Midwest. He values discipline, hard work, modesty, and perseverance—much like my Japanese culture—and tends to downplay compliments. But his snippy and dismissive responses were more likely inherited from his father, who was often curt and dismissive. Though I'd grown accustomed to it, I had never really liked it, and David's frustration resonated with me.

"You know," I said, "you and the second chair violinist were moving in unison, with lots of passion and enthusiasm. I really enjoyed watching you both."

"Thanks, Mom. That's a real compliment." He leaned forward and smiled. "He's a fantastic violinist. I respect him a lot. He should have been the principal violinist but ended up the second chair. I don't know why."

I glanced at Peter as if to say, *See? You've got to be more specific.*

His lips remained pursed.

I'd been looking forward to some pleasant conversation in the car, David enthusiastically sharing with us his music camp experience, me telling him how proud I was to see him make such great progress, and, above all, how relieved I was that he'd made it through such a rigorous boot camp. Instead, we got a sulky teenager in the back seat pining for his newfound love.

As for Liz, something seemed off about her pensive, faraway look, hinting to me she might be a highly sensitive girl. She reminded me of myself at her age. Intuition told me there'd be trouble ahead.

The Japanese Garden

Circa 1960s to early 1980s

When I was four years old, my parents pawned me off to a family friend who was willing to drive me more than an hour each way to a two-year kindergarten, Katabami, in Tokyo. My status-conscious parents sent me there so that I'd have a chance to get into the affiliated elementary school Kunitachi Gakuen, a brutally competitive private school. During the first year, I cried at every drop-off.

Stress didn't end in kindergarten. In second-grade my homeroom teacher was Ms. Sato, a stocky woman in her early thirties with broad shoulders, who looked and acted tough. She was an experienced and effective teacher who was beloved and respected by many students and parents, but whenever I was near her, my body tensed up and my heart raced.

In her class, it was routine before dismissal for the class to recite the multiplication tables in perfect unison. In preparation, we pushed all the desks and chairs to the back of the classroom and lined up in the open area. There were sixty students in the class, so the whole process took time.

One day, I really needed to go to the bathroom when we started but was too intimidated to ask to be excused.

The chant began, "One times one equals one, one times two equals two . . . two times one equals . . ."

I crossed my legs and fought against the urge. I thought I could hold it all the way to the end of nine times nine equals eighty-one, but alas, halfway through, a copious amount of pee gushed out, and I stood over the pool of urine.

"Look, she just peed!" a classmate gasped.

A moment of panicky silence was followed by my loud cry. The chanting abruptly ended as Ms. Sato came over with several rags to clean up the accident. Without saying a word, she held my hand and took me to the nurse's office. My throat tightened. Once in the office, she wiped me clean and gave me a new pair of underwear.

"Okay, you're all set," she said and sent me home. She didn't scold me, and surprisingly, none of my classmates teased or bullied me either.

Still, I was miserable, terribly embarrassed, and humiliated. Those feelings reminded me of my piano recital when I was five. As the curtain rose and I saw a huge crowd, I was so shocked that I froze and stared at them with my mouth wide open. Seconds later, the crowd erupted in laughter. Still sitting in the piano chair, I felt so ashamed. I was on the verge of crying until my teacher came to my rescue. Only this scene burned in my memory; I don't remember anything else, even whether I could play my *Bumblebee* piece at all. On both occasions—from this recital to the pee incident fiascos—I was too young to know the lasting impact of feeling like a failure.

On the train home, I held back my tears, but as I dragged my feet toward the house, tears welled up in my eyes. There'd be no one at home to give me the comfort I longed for after my terrible day. But then I spied Bubu, my sheltie, dashing back and forth beside the chain-link fence, so happy to see me. His exuberant tail-wagging brought a smile back to my face. I kissed his pointy nose through the fence. Bubu was such a gentle, empathetic soul who knew exactly how to cheer me up.

When I went inside, our housekeeper, Hayashi-san, was busy vacuuming, so I went out to play with Bubu in the garden.

Our Japanese garden had a big pond full of floating, white, water lilies. It was immaculately landscaped and maintained by professionals. My father cherished and took great pride in this garden, but he was much too busy to savor it, so I was the greatest beneficiary. Even though my family was absent, at least I had that garden and my dog. This special place brought respite to my anxious mind, and spending hours there with Bubu was my favorite pastime.

The focal point, the large koi pond, contained many jewel-like fish of varying patterns and sizes. Together, they created a fusion of vibrant colors—swirls of gold, silver, red, and orange. When it rained, it was fun to watch them swim to the surface and catch raindrops in their mouths. Even in winter, when the koi hibernated beneath the protective straw mat cover at the far end of the pond, I had great fun breaking the frozen surface with a long bamboo pole while the soapy aroma of winter daphne blossoms wafted in the cold air.

That day, Dad came home and saw me near the pond. "Want to help me feed the koi, Chako?" he asked.

"Sure!" I followed him to the shed, where he grabbed a big bag of fish food. When we got to the pond, he scooped the food into a cup and handed it to me.

"Watch this." He clapped his hands. Immediately, the koi gathered around the main stone landing where we stood. "Go ahead and scatter the food over the water."

When I did, they came right up to the surface and gobbled it all up. These koi were amazingly tame; they let me stroke their heads and playfully nibbled my fingers.

After Dad went back to work, I stayed in the garden and played with Bubu some more. I liked looking at the rocks of variegated browns, grays, and coppers in different shapes and sizes—from boulders to stones the size of sand dollars. I admired the dwarf maple trees with their lacy, burgundy leaves as well as the Japanese irises and the several varieties of azaleas—pink, magenta, yellow, and white. I layered the different colored azaleas on the tip of a chopstick and wrapped it with aluminum foil. Making this magic wand was my spring ritual. I walked around the garden shaking it as I talked to the koi and Bubu, making wishes for happy moments—like more dinners out with my family at the restaurant above the car wash and more family trips to the white sands of Shimoda Beach.

Bubu followed me to the large open area of the garden that showcased vibrant blue and purple hydrangea, spiraea, and a wide variety of trees, such as Japanese maples, birches, and pines. Kimura-san (a family friend who was also my frequent caregiver) was a walking encyclopedia of flowers and trees and taught me the names of almost all the plants in the garden. I was naturally curious and loved plants. I even owned a botany book and enjoyed looking at the pictures.

I went back to the pond to listen to the gentle, trickling sound of the rockery waterfall that fed a steady flow of water into the pond. By the time I'd crossed the blue-gray stone bridge that spanned one end of the pond, the memory of the humiliating experience at school had faded. Between the waterfall and the pump house was a narrow shady path camouflaged by a dense Japanese maple. This was my secret hideaway. I trod through the weeds growing on the berm to get to the end, where a tall, skinny, stone pagoda towered over me.

Next to the pagoda stood a massive blue-gray triangular boulder that had a naturally formed indented ledge just wide enough for me to sit on. From there I surveyed the garden and watched the koi swimming, the water striders skimming over the pond's surface, and the dragonflies hovering above a lily pad, then taking off and landing on another.

I'd always been fascinated by animals. I was three when I went to Sado Island for the funeral of my maternal grandfather, whom I'd never met. I stayed overnight at my grandmother's house and was excited by the sight of a bunch of baby tree frogs stuck on the windows overlooking the rice paddies. My grandmother let me bring one inside. I giggled each time the tiny green frog jumped around and even more when it peed on the tatami mat.

When I was in third grade, my grandmother came to visit us all the way from Sado Island. Her journey took an entire day, including a ferry trip and several long, arduous train rides. Despite that, she brought me a special gift—a red plastic bucket full of tadpoles. I was so surprised and thrilled. She must have remembered my excitement when I'd first seen the tree frogs at her house.

Within days I released the tadpoles into the pond because the bucket looked too crowded. Grandma didn't seem to mind. I didn't realize that my concern for their freedom would end up endangering their lives. Many of them soon disappeared, gobbled up by the koi. The tadpoles that managed to escape that fate, however, turned into frogs and croaked at night through the summer and early fall, long after Grandma had gone home. The sound reminded me of her house and the flooded rice paddies right across the narrow dirt path. I was sad she lived so far away.

At Monkey Bridge

August 14, 2013

Ten days after David returned from music camp and four days before our family trip to northern France, he issued another in a string of requests, for me to drive out of my way so that he and Liz could see each other. This time he wanted me to officially meet both Liz and her mother, Diane, who was bringing Liz to Seattle for her cello lesson.

The woman had to be a saint, driving ninety miles each way to take her daughter into the city twice a week—once for physical therapy and a second time for cello lessons. I accommodated David's request because I thought it was what a good, understanding mother ought to do. My mother had stopped driving me anywhere when I was still in first grade. After she'd had a minor fender-bender, she had decided to become a "paper driver"—retaining her license but never driving. In any case, she refused to do anything she considered too much of a hassle, but lucky for her, she always had someone else to handle chores on her behalf. I didn't.

Usually before a vacation, I felt wired, stressed, and buried in logistics. But this time I'd accomplished everything four days ahead of time and felt relatively calm. I looked forward to meeting and getting to know Liz. David seemed to care deeply about her, so why not meet her mother as well? I proposed to take them out to lunch at Monkey Bridge, my favorite Vietnamese restaurant in Seattle.

When David and I arrived at the restaurant, Liz and her mother were already sitting at a back corner table. When they spotted us, they got up and we shook hands. Liz's long, wavy hair was gathered in the back with a barrette, and she wore a pink T-shirt and jeans. She gave me a warm, friendly smile.

Diane was of medium build, with dark-brown hair cut in a bob. She beamed at us, her smile radiant, eyes sparkling. "I've been so looking forward to meeting you," she said.

We hit it off right away. Even before the waitress came to take our order, we were already immersed in a lively conversation while David and Liz talked quietly to each other.

"Liz is so inspiring," I said to Diane. "I thought she'd been playing cello since she was little, but David told me she started just several years ago. For her to already be at the highest-level orchestra in SYSO, she must be a natural." I stopped short of saying she seemed out of David's league.

"David is also an impressive young man," Diane said. "Liz was telling me about his amazing musicality. You've done a great job raising him."

I had difficulty accepting compliments, whether due to my Japanese upbringing or my personality or maybe both. But for that brief moment, my guard softened and I smiled, instead of refuting it with, *Oh no, it has nothing to do with me. He did it all himself.*

I turned to Liz. "David told me you raised money for music camp by playing your cello on the street. That's gutsy. David would never have done that."

Liz smiled, but David pursed his lips and looked down. *Oh, no.* No matter how long I lived in American culture, my twisted Japanese penchant for self- and family-deprecation was apparently alive and well.

A social-worker-turned-hospice-care professional, Diane was a great listener. While we talked, I glanced at Liz, wondering why she came across as more mature than David and whether she was as fragile as I'd been at her age.

"Liz was born premature," Diane said. "She was so tiny and delicate, it was very challenging to care for her. I became so burned out that I eventually developed postpartum depression."

"Oh my God, that's exactly what happened to me."

The waiter brought us mango salad, spring rolls, and plates of bean sprouts, basil, chilies, and lime for our pho noodle soup. I was so eager to resume my story that I didn't even wait for him to leave. I explained how everything accelerated after my OB/GYN stripped my membranes.

"Within a few days my water broke, and I ended up having a precipitous delivery. Three and a half hours from start to finish. David came out with the umbilical cord wrapped around his neck, and his heart rate went down so rapidly that he had to be extracted by vacuum assistance. I ended up with a third-degree tear and lost lots of blood. The vacuum extraction caused a large hematoma on David's head, which apparently triggered his jaundice. And they asked us to treat him at home for three days under ultraviolet light phototherapy." I took a deep breath. "If I'd given birth in Japan, the hospital would have taken care of it."

Diane was warm and empathetic and reminded me of Dawn Gruen, a pioneer and therapist specializing in postpartum depression. I had sought help from Dawn when David was fifteen months old. My experience didn't quite fit the clinical definition of occurring within four weeks of birth. Instead, the situational stress became recurring and chronic, which, combined with sheer exhaustion and little support, likely led to a delayed onset of postpartum depression.

Dawn was excellent, and I had immediately sensed she understood me when she remarked, "Sounds like you were fairly neglected as a child."

When I started seeing her, she was in remission from lung cancer, and with her help I made lots of progress. But shortly after the recurrence of her cancer, she passed away when David was only two years old. The year before, I'd lost my American host mother, Joanne, to colon cancer. I was absolutely devastated to lose these beloved maternal figures back-to-back.

Following Dawn's passing, I went from one therapist to another but was unable to find anyone nearly as good to replace her. I finally gave up therapy, though I obviously needed it.

Clearly, it had been a while since I'd gotten things off my chest. My stoic Midwestern husband had a tendency to bottle things up with a suck-it-up-and-move-on attitude, and it didn't help that I was in the middle of menopause. But once I started talking to Diane, a torrent of words gushed out, and I couldn't stop myself, no matter how inappropriate it might have been to overshare such personal information during our first meeting. Maybe it was a sign that I needed to see a therapist. David and Liz seemed lost in each other, and though they weren't paying much attention to us, I still caught David's occasional glares. But I ignored them.

The waiter brought us our pho, and we started to eat.

I thought Diane was being a good listener, but maybe she simply couldn't get a word in edgewise. She also appeared slightly uncomfortable with some of the personal details in my incessant chatter, occasionally glancing at David as though gauging his reaction.

I had now launched into a recitation of David's babyhood. "We couldn't sleep a wink, and that was tough. Peter had just started his grueling residency, and I desperately needed to recuperate after giving birth, but we were excited to have our first baby. We didn't expect our sleep deprivation to become so chronic."

While it was painful to recall, I continued to share everything with Diane, my emotions spilling out in a raw, unfiltered torrent. David was an inconsolable, colicky baby, and I struggled with breastfeeding. He had a weird scalp infection that kept returning, along with asthma that required middle-of-the-night nebulizer treatments. There were food allergies and eczema. We were frequent visitors to the Children's Hospital ER, not only because of his asthma but also because of physical injuries, as he was so hyperactive and accident-prone. I'd been aware since he was a toddler that something wasn't quite right, but Peter had dismissed it, saying that David reminded him of when he was a child.

I took a break from my monologue to scoop mango salad into my mouth, barely noticing its sweet, tangy flavor. "When I think of it now," I said, "the tough times began even before David was born."

I sipped some water and thought about when I was thirty weeks pregnant and had relocated from Rochester, Minnesota, to Seattle, driving my small car and following the big U-Haul truck Peter drove for 2,000 miles. My dog Shelly's ashes sat beside me in a box on the passenger seat. Being so fatigued and emotionally labile from wacky pregnancy hormones, I sobbed every time I looked at it.

"This soup is so tasty," Diane said. Maybe it was a subtle hint that she wanted to move on to something more lighthearted. Yet, I couldn't stop. I still felt an urge to release more of my pent-up emotions.

I smiled and then launched into my early years of motherhood misery—especially the lack of access to early maternal support. As we moved on to menopause, I bemoaned how unexpectedly weird and challenging a time it was for me.

Diane's empathic nods and occasional comments were so reassuring that it felt as if I'd crammed years' worth of talk therapy into one lunch. I was so immersed in talking about myself that I almost forgot David and Liz were there. But they were enjoying each other's company so much that they didn't seem to mind being sidelined by our energetic conversation. At one point they got up from the table and said they were going for a walk.

When they stepped out, Diane leaned toward me and lowered her voice, saying, "You know, a few months before Liz met David, she hit rock bottom with her depression and started taking medication. We all scrambled to shore her up."

"Oh my." I knew I'd been right. I wondered what her rock bottom had looked like.

"But ever since she met David, she's been really happy," she said.

"That's great." I smiled half-heartedly as I ripped off a hangnail I'd been picking. My face suddenly felt hot, and despite the air conditioning, I started to perspire. I considered mentioning my hospitalization at age seventeen but managed to avoid bringing up the topic.

On one of the few occasions Diane got a word in, she told me she loved baking, had received training at Le Cordon Bleu North America, and used to own a bakery. She'd had to give it up for a better paying job to support Liz's passion to become a cellist.

"Wow, that's incredible! I admire your commitment!" I was moved by her dedication and willing self-sacrifice. *What about me?* What had I sacrificed as a mother?

I remembered that, in terms of motherhood, my guiding principle had been to do the opposite of my mother, who always put her needs before anyone else's and wouldn't even boil water for me. To be a good, attentive mother, I believed I had to sacrifice everything, including my career and myself, so I admired what Diane had done for her daughter. And yet recently, David had pointed out that I rarely smiled anymore. He was right; I had lost my sense of humor. My life had become joyless.

When David was a toddler, I was working on a book manuscript based on my dissertation, which involved Japanese preschool educators and encouraging childhood spontaneity. An academic press had shown interest, but when they asked to see the completed work, I couldn't seem to finish it. Since then, I'd never fully recovered from the disappointment of letting that opportunity slip through my fingers. Sure, I'd been sleep-deprived, consumed by David's medical issues, and battling postpartum depression, but I should have pushed myself harder. I'd long buried the toxic shame and resentment, with no one to blame except the situation and myself. But the thought that I was failing even at motherhood, the path I'd so eagerly chosen, only depleted my energy and deepened my self-doubt. I felt like nothing.

Diane and I spent more than two hours rambling on—well, I did most of the rambling. I was so engrossed in our conversation that not only did I forget to eat, but I also forgot to keep track of the parking meter. When we left the restaurant, there was a forty-four-dollar parking ticket stuck on my car's windshield.

Diane looked concerned. "Would you like me to cover lunch so that you can take care of that ticket?"

"Oh no, it's okay. I've committed plenty of traffic infractions, so it's long overdue."

Diane laughed. "That's a good way to look at it. I'd be really bummed if I got a ticket like that."

Although I hated the idea of having to pay for the parking violation,

I sucked it up with a smile. Surprisingly, it didn't bother me all that much since our time together seemed well spent. Pouring my heart out to Diane had been more cathartic and cost-effective than talking with a psychiatrist. We shook hands as we parted, and David gave Liz a hug and kissed her on the cheek.

On the way home, David asked, "So what did you think? Did you like them?"

"Oh yes, Liz seems like a very sweet girl. And I really enjoyed meeting Diane."

"I could tell. You were talking a lot about yourself, but Diane's not your therapist, you know."

I winced. "I know. I just needed to get some things off my chest. She was so understanding, and we seemed to have a lot in common." I felt bad for having monopolized the conversation. "But . . ."

"But what?"

"Nothing, never mind." I had enjoyed meeting Liz and talking with Diane. I'd long sought a sympathetic listener who could understand and validate how much suffering I'd endured. It was a part of my identity that I felt entitled to hold on to after all the shit I'd gone through. No matter how misguided that might have been, I was thrilled to have forged a meaningful connection with her. And I had done it the only way I knew how—by revealing my innermost vulnerabilities.

At the same time, I couldn't quite shake the thought that my intuition about Liz had been spot-on; she was indeed a highly sensitive and fragile girl. And the more I thought about it, there was also something amiss about Diane. Her sacrificial spirit of *I'll do anything for my daughter,* was disturbing. It made me feel uncomfortable, but I couldn't figure out why.

I only hoped she wasn't expecting David to become her daughter's knight in shining armor.

Bon Voyage

August 18, 2013

The day arrived for our much-anticipated, two-week family trip to northern France. It had been David's idea. He'd been taking French for five years and wanted to put his language skills into practice. My travel enthusiast husband was all for it. The two of them studied Rick Steves's travel guide for two months to produce an exquisitely detailed itinerary.

David was excited about going but would certainly miss Liz. Looking back on it now, had he met her before all this planning, the trip might never have happened.

I'd extracted myself from family trips for several years, using my menopause-induced fatigue as an excuse. When David first mentioned going to France and Peter agreed, I'd suggested somewhere closer for him to practice his French, like Quebec. But their answer was an unequivocal "*Non.*" When I mentioned that I'd rather stay home, David said, "No, Mom, you've got to come with us this time. I'll be leaving for college soon, and this might be our last chance to travel together."

I wouldn't confess the real reason I didn't enjoy family vacations:

my husband and son were remarkably similar in their personalities, behavior, inattentiveness, and hyperactivity, and I often felt excluded. They liked to cram lots of activities into short periods of time, making everything super hectic and stressful. I'd been trying to balance my family's needs with my own, insisting on downtime by encouraging Peter and David to go on father-son trips. I thought it would be good for them to bond, which it was. What I didn't realize was that it also distanced me further from them.

But David was right. It might be our last chance to vacation together, and things were already kind of rocky with him, so I grudgingly agreed to go along.

Departure day arrived. Immediately, I dreaded the intensity that threatened to engulf me. From the moment Peter and David got up at 6:00 a.m., they were exuberant, zipping around the house like hummingbirds. And what was up with David's selective circadian rhythm anyway? He seemed to have a different body clock operating when readying himself for fun activities like traveling. By contrast, I, who hated both flying and traveling, was behaving like a sloth—just like him on school days. Waiting for the shuttle to take us to SeaTac Airport, I took deep breaths and double-checked my purse to make sure my Xanax was handy. My doctor, who was sympathetic toward my fear of flying, had prescribed it for me. At least I'd found a good pet sitter who could take care of our goofy Biscuit and pain-in-the-butt toy poodle Amber. I reminded myself of Peter's reassuring words, "Don't worry, David and I have got everything worked out. Just relax and come along for the ride."

But when we reached the ticket counter, Peter discovered he'd erroneously entered his name as "Anderson Anderson" instead of "Peter Anderson" while buying the tickets on Expedia. The TSA agent wouldn't let him through because his boarding pass didn't match his ID.

He struggled to maintain his composure. “You guys go ahead,” he said to David and me. “I’ll go back to the counter to correct my ticket and catch up with you at the gate.”

My anxiety shot up. *What if I’m alone with David throughout this trip?* David looked equally shocked. This wasn’t the first time Peter had inconvenienced us because of his carelessness, and my fear was soon mixed with outrage. Not only would I not be able to relax and enjoy a trip that I hadn’t wanted to go on in the first place, but we might also end up fighting the entire time. By the end of this disastrous trip, our relationship would be ruined beyond repair.

Luckily, Peter had put a copy of the itinerary in David’s suitcase, and his last-minute decision to bring his phone was a stroke of luck. (Neither Peter nor I were tech-savvy back then, and I didn’t even own a cell phone, but David did.) Still, I resented having been thrust into a leadership role for which I felt out of practice and ill-equipped.

From that point on, I switched to energy-conservation mode and remained silent in the boarding area. On vacation, I often become a helpless and overly dependent traveler. In the company of a confident traveler, I’d rather remain helpless than lead the expedition and sit back, whine, and complain about the inconvenience, especially when all I wanted to do was stay home and enjoy peace and quiet.

Half an hour later, Peter texted David: “I had to buy a new ticket right on the spot for $2,700 for tomorrow morning because today’s flights are all sold out.”

“Great,” I said. “That totally defeats all the money-saving efforts that made our flight arrangements so complicated in the first place.”

“Mom, calm down.” David read off another message: “We don’t need to pinch euros. There’s enough money to go around. I’ll meet you guys in Paris tomorrow.”

“He’s got to be kidding,” I said. “He trained me to be a cheapskate, and now he's telling me we don't have to be penny-pinchers? Give me a fucking break." I must admit I'm no Mother Teresa and get bitchy under stress. I have a fear of flying and don't like traveling. Period.

"Mom." David lowered his palm down to suggest I take a "chill pill," then he read off the last text from Peter: "I don't want our family to be separated like this ever. I'll rent a temporary phone for us to use while traveling in France, and it'll be waiting for you at the first hotel. And today, David, you've got to step up and be the leader."

He must not have had the stomach to tell me to rise to the occasion after having assured me I could just relax and come along for the ride. With all the adrenaline rushing through me, I didn't have any energy left to stay angry. I slumped in my chair and fell into a zombie-like trance.

"Mom, you look so calm," David said.

Gazing far off, I responded in a monotone. "My stress level has totally maxed out." It was true, and I felt nothing. "Dad's an idiot, and this is such bullshit."

David grimaced, but I didn't care. My crustiness was entirely justified.

The thought of our three-leg flight overwhelmed me: fly to Chicago, a two-hour layover, board a flight to Belgium, another layover, then board a plane to Paris. And then somehow get from Charles de Gaulle Airport to the Hotel Valadon.

When I noticed David's frightened expression, I forced myself to calm down. I took out my portable CD player and put on *The Most Relaxing Piano Album in the World*—a compilation of mellow and romantic works by composers such as Bach, Chopin, Debussy, and Mozart. By the time "Clair de Lune" came up, my initial fight-or-flight response had subsided. My newfound sense of calm helped David relax and take things in stride—at least for a while.

David and I settled into our seats for our Chicago flight, and soon it was time for the routine safety instructions.

"Put on your own oxygen mask first before helping those around you."

Yeah, yeah. I'd heard this so many times. I knew I had to take care of myself first before I could be of any use to others, but I sucked at it.

David and I hadn't traveled alone in a long time. But instead of capitalizing on this opportunity, I couldn't let go of my grudge. "Dad's so careless," I said. "Maybe he has ADHD. I always suspected he had something that makes it hard for him to pay attention. Maybe he can't help it. Maybe—"

David glared at me. "Mom, it's okay to say those things to me but not to Dad. He won't want to be reminded of his mistakes. So please don't, or you'll ruin our trip."

I knew I was putting David in the adult role and weighing him down with too many responsibilities. That day he became my therapist, sounding board, marriage counselor, and travel guide. For the sake of our peace, though, I forced myself to keep my mouth shut. But my anger and frustration continued to simmer.

In a household where breaking and spilling by the hasty and inattentive Anderson *boys* was too common, I had developed a very low tolerance for their carelessness. They were too slow and inefficient, so I'd roll my eyes and rush to clean up their messes before they could even start. Thus, I earned myself the title of domestic tyrant—along with Peter's fury.

"You treat me like a child," he would protest. Sometimes, when I was careless, he'd ask, "How would you react if David or I had done that?"

I knew bickering over seemingly trivial issues was symptomatic of something more serious. But dealing with my marriage seemed like too much work when I was already overwhelmed dealing with David, so I just swept it under the rug. But I knew this wasn't the right thing to do.

Our marriage had been in trouble before. Eight years earlier, I was jolted awake in the middle of the night by a loud, retching noise. I thought Peter had vomited and ran downstairs to get a few towels. But when I returned, something must have happened. He was drooped over the edge of the bed.

"Peter! Peter!" I shouted but got no response. When I tried to prop him up, his face was covered with blood, and blood pooled on his pillow on the floor. He made strange gurgling sounds and seemed like he was in a coma.

I pulled myself together enough to call 911. Luckily our house was less than a mile from a fire station, and within a few minutes paramedics arrived with two fire trucks and an ambulance.

Several husky men entered our house with their big, raggedy boots. *Shoes! Shoes!* I almost shouted.

The paramedics worked in silence, checking Peter's vital signs. They cut his shirt open with scissors, shaved his chest to attach EKG wires, and put an IV into his arm. The tension in the room nearly suffocated me. I was overwhelmed by the fear that he might die.

David woke up and came to the bedroom. "What happened to Daddy?"

I hugged him. "Dad will be okay."

When the procedures were almost done, the lead paramedic asked me a series of questions about Peter's health conditions. "Does he have a history of seizures?"

I didn't know, so I called his parents in Minnesota despite the early hour. It was indeed his first episode of a seizure. By then, Peter had started to regain consciousness but seemed to be in a daze as the leader asked him questions.

"Do you know who she is?" He pointed at me.

"Of course. She's my wife, Shigeko."

"How long have you been married?"

"Umm, three years?"

"No, ten years, Peter! Ten!" I choked up.

I was concerned that he might have lost his memory, but the paramedic reassured me that memory loss after a seizure is often temporary. With the IV still in his arm and wearing only urine-soaked boxer shorts, Peter was escorted downstairs and walked barefoot through a light snow to the ambulance. It was four thirty in the morning. I was going to follow behind the ambulance, but one of the paramedics told me there was no need to rush to the hospital, as it would take the doctors a while to settle him into his room.

By the time David and I left for the hospital two hours later, the snow had accumulated, making the drive treacherous without snow tires. It was scary, but I drove slowly and carefully and managed to reach the hospital without getting into an accident.

When Peter returned home the next day, he told me that a few days before the seizure he'd been talking with a divorce attorney but had decided not to follow through. The seizure had been shocking enough, but this revelation came as even more of a blow.

I knew one of his major complaints in our marriage was my lack of interest in sex. "I can't keep living like this," he often said, or "I'm living in quiet desperation." Still, I couldn't wrap my head around this issue, or maybe I refused to understand it. I was just as unhappy as he was, but divorce had never crossed my mind. I was used to being unhappy. It had been my normal state ever since I was a child. I'd come to view unhappiness as a way of life.

But this? The thought of losing him was devastating. I was outraged by his secrecy, my trust in him shaken.

A few hours into the flight to Belgium, the plane suddenly plunged while going through turbulence, so I popped a Xanax and soon conked out. Hours later when I woke up, David was staring at me, his face frozen in a wide-eyed look of terror. I could almost hear him thinking, *What am I gonna do? I can't depend on Mom.* I smiled and squeezed his hand, hoping to reassure him I wasn't entirely gone.

Once we arrived at Charles de Gaulle Airport, we took the bus to the Paris Opera, then a cab to our hotel. I was mesmerized by the quintessential Parisian architecture—block after block of pale-beige stone buildings with their steeply pitched roofs of blue-gray slate. We drove by the courtyard of the Louvre Museum, passing the large glass pyramid, and I marveled at the perfect harmony of ancient and modern. Stunning. So much historical weight.

It was after four in the afternoon when we finally reached the Hotel Valadon, highly recommended by the Rick Steves guidebook. The hotel was minimalist but clean and well-air-conditioned, and the crisp white linens held a hint of lavender. I flopped down on the bed and couldn't get up—or rather, didn't want to. There was still plenty of daylight, and David wanted to stroll around and then find a place to eat.

"You go on," I said. "I'm not hungry. I need to lie down for a while." I curled up like a child and closed my eyes.

David must have felt a strong urge to take charge (which was uncharted territory for him) because he left and soon returned with a baguette, a ham and cheese sandwich, and a box of Special K with red berries (the French version). I ate a few bites, but I was too tired and tried to go back to sleep.

"Mom, you've got to eat." David's eyes welled up. "This is too much for me. I'm just a kid." Though he had held up pretty well thus far, the stress of having to be the responsible one, in addition to the travel fatigue, must have become too much for him.

"Okay." I took a few more bites even though I didn't feel like eating anything. When I'm stressed, the first thing to go is my appetite. "Don't worry about me. I just need to rest." I was too tired to explain how my menopause might be causing so much fatigue. I also thought he wouldn't understand it anyway.

A couple of hours later, I was jolted awake by David screaming in his sleep. I touched his foot gently and said, "It's just a dream." He didn't wake up, but he stopped screaming. I took a shower, washed my hair, and felt refreshed and ready to go again.

"Hey, if you want to walk around," I said, "I'll come with you."

"No, it's too much effort," he said angrily and went back to sleep.

I felt sad knowing how much he'd been looking forward to this trip. *It doesn't have to be this way*, I thought. *When Peter gets here tomorrow, everything will be fine.*

After David woke up two hours later, we went to the front desk to ask for the phone Peter had reserved for us. I asked the main receptionist, who spoke English well, "Is it safe for us to walk around here at night?"

"Oh yes, it's safe. Don't worry, people here are not walking around with their guns," she said and gestured as if holding a machine gun. *Oh my.* I gave her a wry smile, not expecting to be reminded of America's gun culture.

Peter arrived the next morning after breakfast. We were all relieved to be together again. David and I kept him company while he ate, and he looked especially happy and energized to see us. He'd been so anxious he hadn't slept at all that night on the plane.

I should have left it at that, but I'd already started the trip off on the wrong foot. And that set the tone for the rest of it. No matter how hard I tried to shake it off, my grudge lingered, especially when Peter made more careless mistakes with that devil-may-care attitude of his. But for the sake of family peace, I refrained from interjecting my opinions or suggestions about what to do.

For the next three days, we toured Paris. Peter and David insisted on visiting the Louvre and Versailles. I'd already seen them both thirty years earlier during a youth European tour.

"They can't have changed all that much," I said. "You guys go ahead."

"Mom," David said, "you're ruining this trip."

"Hey, you guys forced me to come." *Come for the ride.* Those had been Peter's words. "This hasn't been easy for me. Any more pressure and I'll get bitchy, so don't even try."

Moments later, I felt bad. "I'm sorry. I'm just wiped out. Give me some time to recuperate, and I'll join you." I vacillated between feeling guilty about not going and having a fierce desire to shout, *You forced me to come here against my will! Just leave me alone and let me have some peace and quiet!* I struggled to snap out of my mood. I didn't feel like myself anymore. I felt out of control. My mind kept returning to the night of Peter's seizure and the thought of him hiring a divorce lawyer. It colored everything.

The next day, we walked all over Paris. It was a hot, muggy day, and after climbing partway to the top of the Arc de Triomphe where we had a panoramic view of Paris, I spotted a bench where I could sit and rest. David was trying to capture a perfect image of the intricate spiral staircase, and Peter strolled around the exhibit area.

Next to me sat a friendly looking older couple from Australia. The woman had a twinkly smile. We struck up a conversation about the recent catastrophic wildfires in Australia and how they were affecting the wild animals. We discussed wallabies (I'd long harbored a secret desire to have a pet wallaby), and she mentioned having lived in Japan. It was a welcome respite from keeping up with the two high-energy Andersons. I was also dying to speak English with other people. This was what I valued about traveling: not the whirlwind itinerary but the serendipitous interactions with total strangers, how, by simply striking up a casual conversation, we discovered mutual interests and respect for each other's cultures.

The next day was the beginning of our road trip to northern France, which meant striking out on our own to find the Europcar rental location. This proved to be a bit of a challenge. We first had to find our way around the Paris Metro, which was quite complicated and hectic and reminded me of Tokyo. We trekked down super-long corridors, climbing up and then down seemingly endless staircases. Once on the train, we discovered we were going in the wrong direction and had to go all the way back, schlepping our luggage.

So far, nothing on this trip had gone without a hitch, but all the mishaps up to that point had just been a warm-up. Once we left Paris, it got worse.

We were off to Rouen and Ouistreham. Peter knew how to drive a stick shift, so I rode shotgun. My job was to stay alert for our easily distractible driver and manage his left-right confusion. It took us forever to get out of Paris, not only because of the traffic but also because the roads were so confusing.

"Didn't we just see this building with the grass roof half an hour ago?" I remarked. And a bit later, unhelpfully, "Here we are right back at the same spot for the third time."

For the first hour and a half, all we heard from our GPS was "Recalculating," as we missed several of our turns. I tried to refrain from sarcastic comments—they would only exacerbate Peter's temper—but it wasn't easy.

Two hours into this escapade, I couldn't take it anymore. After a brief stop at a convenience store, I politely excused myself and insisted that David become the navigation assistant. Then I took a back seat. Literally.

After that, things operated relatively smoothly—in the car.

At every hotel check-in, David had to make sure we had Wi-Fi access so that he could contact Liz. Invariably, it didn't work properly, which made him frustrated and angry. Almost every day, they coordinated time to Skype. They planned to record a piano and cello duet of Rachmaninoff's "Vocalise" after David got home and post it on YouTube. I'd heard this hauntingly beautiful, melancholy piece on his computer ad nauseam, and in my mind it became the theme music for our trip.

David kept insisting on buying souvenirs for Liz, and I ended up having to pay for them. He had inherited this romantic and thoughtful attribute from Peter. I, of course, could have (and should have) said no, but I didn't have the stomach for his sulky moods. Every few minutes, he'd say, "Liz would love this," or "I wish Liz were here." I wasn't the only one who wasn't living in the moment.

But there were also many high points to the trip.

Our pilgrimage to the Normandy American Cemetery was so moving that Peter and I both became teary-eyed. It was a blustery day with a steady drizzle, and the row after row of white crosses against the gray sky was somber. The highlight of the entire trip for me, however, was Mont Saint-Michel. We stayed in the village at the foot of the ancient abbey and felt as if we'd slipped back into medieval times.

We took a self-guided candlelight tour of the historic monastery as classical music performed by a flautist, harpist, and cellist echoed through the chambers. Its awe-inspiring penthouse cloister was my favorite place of all. I could easily imagine devout monks praying and taking meditative walks in the ancient past. I was so glad to have this shared experience with Peter and David and felt closer to them.

The next morning, after checking out of the historic hotel, it was time for our much-anticipated family photo op with the backdrop of Mont Saint-Michel. Peter and David had long been planning to use this photo for our Christmas card. Since I'd opted out of family vacations for many years, this was a once-in-a-blue-moon opportunity. For someone who'd grown up with no such photos, I didn't understand why we should make such a fuss about it. The day was extremely windy, and the wind kept knocking down David's camera stand. It took a couple dozen attempts to get a satisfying shot, but I'd run out of patience by then. Their goal to capture the spirit of family togetherness had become a nuisance. While Peter and David both looked happy in the photo, I wore sunglasses and a half-hearted smile, neither of which fully hid my fatigue and irritation.

As our road trip drew to a close, my breathing became calmer—a sign of relief—but that was precisely when the ultimate scare happened. We were searching for a gas station so that we could return the car with a full tank, but the GPS directions were so confusing we were cutting it close to the deadline for bringing back the car. Amidst all the commotion, Peter wasn't paying full attention as he turned left to enter the parking garage just as a bicyclist suddenly appeared in front of us on the sidewalk.

"Bicycle!" I screamed, and he screeched to a stop.

For a moment, I was speechless. "You almost ran over that cyclist!"

"Oh no, I saw him," Peter said. "I wasn't going to run him over."

"No, you would have hit him if I hadn't screamed!" My heart was still pounding, but there was no point arguing with him. Instead, I thanked God for sparing the cyclist and patted myself on the back for my alertness.

After returning our car, we headed to the apartment in Montmartre we'd rented from a Frenchman named Pierre, where we were to stay for the remaining three days. But I had little recollection of how I got there. Peter told me we took the metro, but I must have been too dazed to register, a delayed post-adrenaline effect after our near miss. This seemed to be a crucial difference between the rest of my family and me: my fight-or-flight-or-freeze response hung on long after a crisis passed. The apartment was two blocks from Sacré-Cœur, the focal point of a neighborhood known for over a century as a hangout for artists, writers, and prostitutes, as well as a center for all sorts of seedy activities (and home of the Moulin Rouge).

A block away from our apartment in Montmartre, there was a restaurant that served a delectable combination of croque monsieur and a butter lettuce salad with a simple vinaigrette. Since we'd all enjoyed it so much, the next evening while I was resting, Peter and David went back to order takeout. Although the servers initially said they weren't set up for takeout, they offered to accommodate us if we brought our own plates. So, Peter and David came back to the apartment for some plates, then returned a few minutes later with our dinner. After so many meals at restaurants, it was relaxing to eat dinner in the privacy of the apartment. We savored it.

Ever since Peter first watched *Pulp Fiction* in 1994 and heard about a "Royale with cheese" (i.e., Quarter-Pounder with cheese) and ordering beer at a French McDonald's, it had become his mission to make a pilgrimage to a French McDonald's. As soon as we stepped into a McDonald's in Paris, he tried to take a photo of the menu listing the Royale with cheese, but alas, the manager thwarted his attempt. David was later able to discreetly snap a picture of Peter eating his Royale with cheese and holding a small can of Heineken.

I can still hear him saying, "Royale with cheese." I loved how Peter, this down-to-earth, modest man, found happiness in something so silly and small. I wished the whole trip had felt this light and easy.

The next day, while lying down in energy-conservation mode with my eyes closed, I eavesdropped on my husband and son's conversation.

"I want to visit Liz in Bellingham the morning after we get home," David said. "I checked the Greyhound Bus schedule, and I can catch the 8:00 a.m. bus downtown. It'll get me to Bellingham around ten-ish."

I was flabbergasted. We wouldn't get into SeaTac until 1:30 a.m., which meant by the time we got home and went to bed, it would probably be around 3:00 a.m. And he was talking about taking the 8:00 a.m. bus from downtown, which meant someone had to take him there. I expected Peter to say something to that effect.

Instead, he said, "Yeah, that shouldn't be a problem. I'll take you to the bus station."

What? Enough was enough. I was fed up with my impulsive and obsessive son and clueless husband. I don't claim to be the world's most rational person, but this time I felt instinctively that I was right. "Pardon me, and excuse my French, but are you guys fucking kidding me? What are you thinking? You'll be exhausted."

David and Peter stared at me, mouths open.

It didn't even slow me down. "It's dangerous to be on a public bus when you're so tired. You can get mugged, or shot, or maybe even . . . eaten by a crazy person." I recalled the horror story from 2008 on a Greyhound bus in Canada, when a mentally unstable passenger had decapitated and cannibalized a fellow passenger.

"You have absolutely no common sense," I said. "Neither of you."

The two of them fell silent. It was a rare moment: I got to have the final word *and* I felt sure about myself.

The trip was so stressful at times that it strained my patience. And when I was crabby, the thought occasionally crossed my mind about how much easier my life would be without that knucklehead Peter. It wasn't until much later that I realized I had successfully managed to ruin what could have been a perfectly good family vacation.

My Sixteenth Birthday

July 16, 1977

On the day I turned sixteen, I left my family for an entire month to go to America for the first time. It was the summer that *Star Wars* became a worldwide blockbuster hit. I was one of seven students from a weekend English language school to participate in a homestay program in Napa, California, and attend an ESL course at Napa Junior College. As my surgeon father was performing an appendectomy, and my mother, the socialite Imelda Marcos of Sagamihara, was out shopping for her twentieth pair of Ferragamo shoes, I was pawned off to my father's hospital employee, who drove me three hours to the new Narita Airport.

On the flight to California, every time we hit a pocket of turbulence I clutched the arms of my seat, closed my eyes, and thought about meeting my host mother. From the letter Joanne had sent me, I imagined her with a warm, cheerful smile. The thought of meeting the Schmidt family slowed my breathing and loosened the knot in my stomach.

As soon as we landed, everyone shuffled toward customs and then into the baggage claim area, but I was full of energy. People passing by smiled at me. Some even said, "Hi," and I returned their greeting. People laughed and hugged and kissed each other. The friendly atmosphere was such a contrast to Japan, where most people typically avoid eye contact. The Japanese are private people, but this is also a form of self-preservation from the sensory overload that comes from living in crowded conditions.

At the gate, Mrs. Schmidt immediately recognized me from the photo I'd sent her and introduced herself and her second son, Ricky. Joanne was an attractive, middle-aged woman with a radiant smile, short brown, curly hair, slightly wrinkled tanned skin, and intense brown eyes. She came across as understated and down-to-earth, but there was also something elegant and sophisticated about her. Through our correspondence, she told me she'd earned a PhD in music and was teaching at Napa Junior College. Ricky, twenty-one, was a handsome man with blond hair, stunning blue eyes, and a gentle smile. He reminded me of Steve McQueen.

"So glad you're finally here," said Joanne.

I shook her hand and told her to call me Chako. I was not yet fluent in English but spoke enough to get by.

As we stepped outside the terminal and walked toward Ricky's car, a cool, invigorating wind struck me. I felt giddy with anticipation. "Today is my birthday." I grinned. "I'm sixteen."

"Happy birthday!" they said, smiling. My family never celebrated birthdays, so their exuberant good wishes were a heartening surprise.

They stopped next to a beat-up Chevy pickup riddled with dents and rust spots. It looked like it might have been white once. *Oh my God, what kind of car is this?* In her letter, Joanne had mentioned that everyone in the family was either a graduate of, or was currently attending, Stanford, which my tutor told me was an elite school. I hadn't gotten the impression they were poor. *I hope I won't end up sleeping on a couch in the living room all month.* But I hid my uneasiness behind a twitchy smile.

As Ricky slid behind the wheel, Joanne nudged me onto the bench seat from the passenger side, and she followed after me. I felt a bit awkward sandwiched between them, but I liked their immediate closeness and held my breath, not wanting to ruin this intimate moment.An hour later, we arrived in Napa and drove through the countryside. The scenery was breathtaking. Row after row of lush green vines, tethered to wooden posts and trained along trellises, sprawled over the sunlit hillsides. I was spellbound, imagining this must be the closest place to heaven. At last, Ricky steered the pickup into the driveway between tall, neatly sheared evergreen hedges, up to a charming, one-story, lavender-blue house with white trim and a gray roof. Not small, but not big either.

I marveled at the front garden with its massive, dark-red geraniums and white alyssums planted along the front borders. There were almond, plum, and peach trees. We parked behind the house, and that was when I saw Mr. Schmidt's red Porsche 911 Carrera—almost identical to my brother's—parked under the carport. With that touch of familiarity, I put my previous concern to rest. I was young and financially too sheltered and entitled to know any better.

Joanne pointed to the raspberry and blackberry patches in the backyard and told me to help myself to the berries anytime I wanted. I'd never eaten either fruit and could hardly wait to taste them.

Inside, the house was spacious, inviting, and brighter than my cluttered, chaotic, two-story house in Japan, which I associated with darkness, oppression, and isolation. Ricky led me through the narrow hallway, carrying my luggage to the room Joanne had prepared for me. The room, kitty-corner from the bathroom, belonged to the youngest in the family, Cynthia, who was away that summer studying at the Goethe-Institut in Germany. Her room was small and cozy, with a window overlooking the front yard. There was a desk and a bookshelf with many trophies displayed.

I opened the closet to put my stuff away and hesitantly moved Cynthia's clothes to the side to make space for mine. A few tennis rackets leaned against the back of the closet wall. I later learned she was among the best collegiate tennis players in the state, hence all the trophies. On top of the dresser was a dainty flower arrangement of light pink roses, pansies, and white alyssums from the garden. I bent forward and inhaled their sweet fragrance.

Joanne stopped by and showed me how to turn on the electric blanket in case I got cold at night.

I was startled. "In Japan, we never use an electric blanket during the summer. We keep the air conditioner on nonstop."

"It does get cold here at night," Joanne said. She also explained the water restrictions in drought-stricken California and told me to keep my showers short.

Their family structure was identical to mine. Like me, Cynthia had two older brothers. Ricky, majoring in religion at Stanford, was five years older than I was. Eric, who'd just graduated and was away practicing meditation at Green Gulch Farm Zen Center, was seven years my senior. Joanne told me I'd have a chance to meet him sometime later during my one-month stay. I wished I could stay much longer. Already I longed to be part of this family and naively pictured myself filling Cynthia's spot for the summer.

Joanne suggested that I rest a bit after the long day, so I decided to lie down.

I awoke to a gentle knock on the door. I jumped out of bed, feeling disoriented. It was 5:30 p.m.

"Richard's back," Joanne said, "and he'd like to meet you. And dinner's almost ready."

I flashed back to evenings at home when the housekeeper, Hayashi-san, called me to dinner before she left at 5:30 p.m. She was a kind and gentle old lady but kept herself at arm's length. Before leaving, she would set dinner on the kitchen table. Her repertoire of entrées was shockingly small, and the same dishes would reappear every five days or so. I'd sit down in front of the TV with her signature potato croquette. She'd bring me a cup of *hojicha* (roasted green tea) as I shoveled food smeared with Bull-Dog *tonkatsu* sauce into my mouth. While eating, I often watched her hurrying to leave. As soon as the apprehension of being alone kicked in, I could no longer savor the food.

I was eager to see what kind of dinner I would have with my American family. I checked myself in the mirror and combed my unruly hair.

My host father, Richard Schmidt, was a busy stockbroker. He stood next to the kitchen table, reading the newspaper through black-rimmed glasses. He seemed to be in his late forties—about six feet tall, slightly heavyset, and balding. He looked dignified in his dark-gray suit and had the aura of a self-assured executive. As soon as he saw me, he grinned, his eyes twinkling. "You must be Chako!" he said in a deep baritone.

I approached him with a casual, "Nice to meet you," but my voice was nervous and my hands shaky. He gave me a firm, strong handshake. A bit overpowering at first.

"Dinner's ready," Joanne said. "We're eating in the backyard tonight."

Richard excused himself to change clothes. I helped by carrying the large wooden bowl of salad made with freshly picked vegetables from the garden—lettuce, carrots, peas, tomatoes, and radishes—to the picnic table where Ricky was setting out napkins and utensils. I placed the bowl in the center. Joanne brought out a platter of grilled steaks, and we all sat down to eat.

The salad was absolutely the best I'd ever eaten. The delicious homemade vinaigrette dressing was slightly sweet and tangy and perfectly complemented the salad. Joanne later taught me the recipe—olive oil, balsamic vinegar, a bit of Dijon mustard, a touch of honey, and hints of rosemary, peppermint, basil, and oregano.

"So, you turned sixteen today, huh?" Richard asked.

"Yes," I said.

"Happy birthday, sweet sixteen!" he said.

I didn't know what that meant, but I smiled and said, "Thank you."

During dinner, Richard's dignified low voice and the way he talked reminded me of Jack Nicholson, and I saw some resemblance in his appearance as well. I also learned that Joanne was a masterful violinist who not only taught music and violin but was also the maestro of the Napa Valley Symphony Orchestra. That explained her intelligence and calm self-confidence.

I told them all about my fascination with American slang. The very first slang I'd learned was from a local American girl living on a nearby military base.

"What is it?" Richard asked.

"Jive turkey."

They all burst out laughing.

Richard then taught me some more useful idiomatic expressions, like "eager beaver," "hogwash," and "a bunch of baloney," and Ricky wrote them down for me.

After the delicious dinner, Joanne and Ricky cleared the table. When they returned from the kitchen, Joanne carried a birthday cake, and Ricky followed with dessert plates and forks.

I was speechless. It was a homemade angel food cake decorated with whipped cream and topped with sliced strawberries and raspberries. Ricky lit the sixteen candles, and they sang "Happy Birthday." I was so touched my eyes welled up. My joy was complete.

The only birthday celebration I could remember was back in second grade. It was an exciting event that a dozen classmates had attended from far away. We'd had catered food and ate strawberry shortcake. I was overjoyed to see my classmates outside of school for the first time, even though none of my family members were there.

"Okay, Chako," Richard said, "blow out those candles and make a wish."

At first, I didn't know what to wish for, but as I blew out the candles, I closed my eyes. *I wish for happiness.*

The next morning, I awoke before 7:00 a.m.—too early for a sleepyhead like me, still heavily jet-lagged. I felt a bit dizzy. Part of me wanted to stay in bed all morning, but I forced myself up because I didn't want to waste precious time with the family.

I shivered as I changed into a T-shirt and jeans and slipped my bare feet into red canvas sneakers. Joanne was right. It did get cold during the night. I wished I'd brought some warm clothes. Outside, dense fog enveloped the landscape. The gray, fall-like atmosphere starkly contrasted with the azure sky and sparkling rays of sunshine I'd seen the day before.

Rubbing my sleepy eyes, I shuffled down the narrow hallway. As soon as I stepped into the kitchen, Joanne greeted me cheerfully.

"Good morning, Chako. I hope you slept well. How about some breakfast?"

The round wooden table bore a charming arrangement of delicate jasmines, alyssums, and pansies surrounded by a plate of homemade whole wheat bread, jars of honey and raspberry jam, a bowl of plain yogurt, and peaches and raspberries freshly picked from the backyard. There was also a large glass jar filled with a golden cereal I'd never seen before.

"It's called granola," Joanne said.

I must have looked confused because she then explained what it was. "All my children like it. I also have oatmeal on the stove if you'd prefer."

"Oh no, I want to try this."

I observed how she ate her granola. She put peach slices on top, poured milk onto it, and ate, making a crunching noise. I followed suit. It was a complex blend of textures and sweet, nutty flavors. I couldn't remember the last time I'd eaten anything this wholesome and yummy. What a contrast it was to my usual boring breakfast of buttered white toast and lemon tea.

After Joanne finished her breakfast, she sipped her peppermint tea to keep me company while I ate. Three semi-sepia-toned portraits of her children hung on the wall. The pictures had been taken when her kids were in grade school. On the very left was the oldest, Eric, who appeared smart and had a mischievous smile. Ricky appeared shy with a bashful smile that reflected his sensitive nature. Cynthia looked bright and self-assured. I could tell how proud Joanne was of each of them. I looked at those portraits with envy. A display like this might have been a common American tradition, but to me it was a stark reminder of my home, where there were no such family pictures.

Outside the large kitchen window hung a flower basket with pretty, bright-pink-and-purple, pendant-like flowers.

"It's a fuchsia," Joanne told me, following my gaze.

Suddenly a tiny bird appeared, zipping from flower to flower, sticking its beak into each blossom.

"A hummingbird," Joanne said. "My favorite."

I watched it for a while, admiring its dark-green iridescent sheen.

Unlike me, Joanne was a woman of few words, and there were awkward silences now and then, but her smile was reassuring. Her presence wrapped me with a warm and gentle energy.

I was moved and suddenly choked up. "You . . . your children are very lucky to have such a wonderful mother." My throat constricted.

She looked baffled. "But surely you have a wonderful mother too."

I'd almost forgotten about my mother and didn't want to think of her now that I was here with this new family. "She's not around much."

"She must just be really busy," Joanne said.

By the time I was in second or third grade I had become quite used to coming home to a house where only Hayashi-san was there, tending to the chores.

"Where's Mom?" I'd ask.

"I don't know," she'd say. "I think she went out with her friends. Might be home late."

Over the years, "Where's Mom?" became a mundane rhetorical question also used by my father and two brothers. No one seemed to care about the answer. It was more like a way of greeting each other. After Hayashi-san scurried home at 5:30 p.m. each evening, the silence and empty space loomed large. I often sat down in the front hallway with Bubu to wait for my mom. When tears rolled down my cheeks, he licked them away.

"Yes, you're right," I said to Joanne, "she *is* busy." I took another bite of granola, savoring it. When I swallowed, my throat was still tight.

Joanne's kitchen was practical but also pretty. There was a flour mill she kept for grinding her own flour. An assortment of healthy snacks—dried apricots and dates, almonds, and nectarines—sat on a wooden plate next to the stove. She'd pick the lovely, light-pink roses, white, sweet alyssum, and lavender from her garden and arrange them in a white ceramic vase on the table. It was the home of a family, well cared for and filled with love.

After an awkward silence, I said, "This granola tastes wonderful. Would you share the recipe?"

"Of course." She placed her warm hand on mine.

I'd make it for myself when I got home. I pictured the earthy cereal filling a large gleaming glass jar on the kitchen table next to the wicker basket of *shokupan*, the square loaf of white bread that was a permanent fixture in our house. I imagined pouring my creation into a rustic wooden bowl just like Joanne's, then topping it with slices of fresh, juicy peaches and a splash of cold milk. I'd savor each bite—the slightly browned oats, sweet, crunchy nuts, California raisins, and hint of molasses—the flavors lingering on my tongue long after I rushed to school, wishing I were back in Napa.

Familial Culture Shock

September 1977 to February 1979

When I returned to Japan, no one from my family was at the airport to pick me up, so my best friend's mother gave me a ride home. The house in Sagamihara was empty. I put a piece of white bread into the toaster oven and turned on the timer. The only sound in the kitchen was the ticking of the oven. My feelings of isolation, disconnection, and estrangement were suddenly almost unbearable.

For a few years, I'd been following in the steps of my oldest brother by giving my mom the silent treatment as an act of protest and defiance against her. But after returning from California, I became increasingly confrontational, argumentative, and belligerent toward my mom. Our differences in values and priorities became too obvious to ignore. I longed for substance, empathy, and compassion, and I thought family should be my mother's top priority. But she cared too much about her external appearance and maintaining a charismatic public persona while totally neglecting the family and her parental responsibilities. Coming to a mutual understanding with her about anything was next to impossible, so I gave up on even having a dialogue with her.

One night while I was washing my face before going to bed, Mom came home. Her face was red, and I smelled alcohol on her breath. Without saying a word, she conked out on the living room floor. When Dad came home some time later, I tried nudging her with my foot.

"Hey, wake up!" When she didn't respond, I said louder, "Get up and keep Dad company." When she still didn't respond, an intense anger and resentment exploded inside me. I kicked her and said, "Look at you. Dad comes home after working all day, and you can't even warm up his dinner." Warm it up? She hadn't even cooked it. Hayashi-san was the one who'd prepared it.

Without saying anything, Mom slowly and reluctantly got up, shuffled into the kitchen, and warmed up Dad's food. She managed to stick around for several minutes with her eyes half-closed while he ate, and then went right back to sleep on the living room floor. It was infuriating, but what was so sad and heartbreaking was that Dad just took it and said nothing. By then, he must have given up.

During the winter when I was seventeen, a year and a half after coming back from California, I finally realized it was crazy to try to understand my family's issues. I couldn't change them no matter how hard I tried, so why bother? I was so tired of being disappointed, and my pent-up feelings of anger, resentment, and frustration were destroying me. It seemed easier to give up and distance myself altogether.

I decided to do everything in my power to take control of my life (except financially) because it was clear that I couldn't depend on my parents—especially my mother. I got myself up every morning, ate the granola I made from Joanne's recipe, and left home early to go to school so that I could enjoy a leisurely walk to the train station. No more adrenaline rush from panic, no more last-minute pleas to my father to drive me to the station.

My parents, who'd been mostly uninvolved in my life, noticed these drastic changes and became hypervigilant, trying to micromanage me. They'd dissuade me from staying up late and getting up early or taking a bath too often because it would strip the natural oil from my skin.

"Leave me alone!" I'd yell with more conviction than I'd ever shown before.

I blew up at my mom at the slightest provocation. One day, we got into yet another heated argument when I complained about her behavior and expressed sympathy for Dad's loneliness.

"What an ungrateful, spoiled brat you've become!" Mom shouted at me in the hallway. "You used to be quiet and obedient. What's gotten into you? I didn't raise you this way."

I stood at the bottom of the stairs. Beside me was a mound of something covered by a large cloth. New purchases? I hated everything about the messy house with all that suffocating clutter. "You didn't raise me at all. I raised myself with the help of surrogate parents."

"Don't you dare talk back to me like that. Ever since you came back from America you've changed for the worse. That was the biggest mistake we ever made to let you go there."

That was too much. How could she say my happiest summer was the biggest mistake?

In the midst of this argument, Dad came home for lunch from the hospital.

"Dad, Mom's crazy," I blurted. "You've got to divorce her."

Mom was so shocked that her legs gave out on her. Dad caught her before she hit the floor.

"How dare you say such awful things?" Dad said. "Apologize to your mother."

I had somehow expected Dad to side with me. Ever since I'd witnessed the horrific scene when he'd fought with Mom like a monster, there hadn't been any physical violence between them, but I assumed Dad still despised Mom. Feeling disappointed and rejected, I stomped upstairs to my room and slammed the door. I sobbed, feeling more alone than ever. No one would side with me.

One day when both of my parents were out of town, I called Ms. Iida, a retired office worker from my dad's hospital. I'd had a few other caregivers, but I was particularly attached to Ms. Iida as she'd taken care of me during my formative years as if I were one of her own.

"Thank you for being so good to me for all these years," I said. "I'll never forget your kindness." Then I hung up.

My sense of despair at not being able to count on my family fueled my desire to find the meaning, truth, and purpose of life. I stayed up hours past bedtime reading the Bible, *Zen Mind, Beginners Mind* (Ricky had sent it from California), and a few other religious and philosophical books. I did the same the next night and the next. I was addicted, hyper-engaged. With almost no sleep, I'd then head to school. Before I knew it, a week had gone by.

One morning on my walk to school, I reached an epiphany. All I had to do was follow God and everything would be fine. I'd attained *satori* (enlightenment), or so I thought. I felt as if I'd transcended my ego and been set free. Suddenly I was euphoric—maybe too happy. But it didn't end there. I had stopped eating, not because I was becoming anorexic but because I simply wasn't hungry. And the more my family tried to force me to eat, the harder I resisted. I refused to let them exert their will over me.

My parents insisted that I go to the hospital and get checked over, but I remained defiant and told them there was nothing wrong with me. What I didn't realize until later was that the euphoria I experienced was also a warning sign of a manic episode. But of course, I didn't know then that it was also an inevitable consequence of a week-long sleep deprivation.

Instead, I mistook the tremendous energy I felt as a result of my newfound enlightenment. I got up ridiculously early and biked everywhere, which made me feel alive and free. One morning, I even biked all the way to see Ms. Iida in Machida, although I'd never biked there before. It took me nearly two hours. I also started to hallucinate while listening to FEN (the Far East Network, an American military radio station) and thought Wolfman Jack was talking directly to me through the radio.

But I thought I was fine.

Locked Up

February 1, 1979 to March 30, 1979

One day in early February when I was seventeen, my brother Hiro-chan entered my bedroom carrying a syringe. Hiro-chan was a doctor, so it wasn't that unusual. But still—

"What's that for?" I was lying on my bed resting.

His face characteristically stern, he blinked rapidly and said, "Not to worry. It'll help you relax."

I rolled over. "Don't need it, don't want it." Then I felt a prick in my arm.

That was the last thing I remembered.

When I woke up, I had no idea where I was. I felt so disoriented, as if I had temporary amnesia. And because I was moving in and out of lucid dreams, I confused reality with those dreams. I could tell I was in a hospital, though I had no idea how I'd gotten there or why I was there. I thought I was in a TV medical drama production studio, and everyone else was a cast member.

An attractive pregnant woman in her thirties—short, curled hair, a small oval face, and pretty, dark eyes—wearing a white coat sat in the chair next to my bed. She introduced herself as Dr. Asano and said she would be in charge of my care. What care? I was still in a dreamy state and thought she was the weather bimbo sent from a local TV station. I didn't take any of her questions seriously and gave nonsensical answers. After a while, she gave up and left.

When a nurse came to check on me, she told me I was at the Yokohama Harbor Medical Center, two hours from home. She said I'd been so heavily sedated that I'd slept off and on for several days, and since I wasn't eating, I had been fed through a nasogastric tube. I started piecing together what might have happened. Hiro-chan had given me a tranquilizer. The realization devastated me. Hiro-chan: the only family member I trusted. Now there was no one left who I could trust. I felt totally alone in this world.

The nurse told me I'd tried getting up to go to the bathroom multiple times, of which I had no recollection. She told me that sometimes I passed out, and they'd find me on the bathroom floor. As she jotted down something in my chart, memories of the past few days surfaced. While sleeping, I'd experienced a sudden, sharp pain in my vagina as if stabbed by a shard of glass. "Ouch!" I cried, and the pain went away. The memory was so unusual and vivid that I knew I hadn't dreamed it.

My room had a radio, a toaster, and a few pieces of silverware sitting on the nightstand. Inside the closet there was a white T-shirt, a pair of jeans, slippers, two sets of new pajamas, and a pink, plush, velvet robe. The nurse said my mom had brought them while I slept.

"Go check out your food," she said. There was a fridge and freezer in front of the nurses' station. "Your mom went on a shopping spree and brought you lots of goodies."

I didn't understand why she had brought me so much stuff. I was ready to leave immediately. I felt convinced that I was merely holding the hospital bed for her since she was the one who should be hospitalized. I'd seen enough of her erratic, irrational, and irresponsible behavior over the years. She was the crazy one.

Still a bit dizzy and lightheaded, I put on the pink velvet robe and made my way to the nurses' station. Inside the fridge I found nectarines and a loaf of whole wheat bread, which I'd become fond of since my visit to Napa. In the freezer were two half-gallons of my favorite brand of ice cream, one chocolate and one strawberry.

While I inspected the food items with my name on them, another nurse came by and said, "Why don't you forgive your mother? She's been here so often. She's working very hard to make it up to you."

"No! Never!" I said. "I hate her!" I slammed the fridge door and stomped off to my room to grab a spoon.

I returned to the fridge, took the chocolate ice cream from the freezer, and ate it straight from the container. At the nurses' station I leaned against the counter, devouring the ice cream, and asked why I had to be there and when I could go home.

"You have such bad manners," one of the nurses said. "Why don't you eat the ice cream in a bowl?"

"There are no bowls in my room." I kept eating, ignoring her. I didn't learn until later that behavior like this was interpreted as a negative sign and would be written up, prolonging my hospital stay.

One day I was hanging out in front of the nurses' station, asking the same questions, "Why am I here? When can I return home?"

The head nurse casually said, "I don't know why you're complaining. Dr. Hasegawa even gave you a bath while you were sleeping."

What? Doctors don't bathe patients. Nurses do. And he wasn't even my doctor.

By that point, I knew who Dr. Hasegawa was. He looked more like a *chinpira* (a low-level *yakuza* or gangster) than a legitimate doctor. He had tanned skin with acne scars and unnatural-looking short, coiled hair as if it were permed. Behind his blue-tinted glasses were lecherous eyes. His creepy smile repelled me.

Whether the nurse had mentioned this inadvertently or on purpose, I couldn't tell, but I didn't press her any further. My head was too messed up from all the meds. Thoughts swirled: *How could that possibly happen? How could anyone let it happen? Why had I needed a bath when I was in a vegetative state? And why was she telling me this now?*

When I suddenly connected the dots between my sharp vaginal pain and the bath, I turned into a vengeful bull ready to charge. I felt violated and outraged and found the hospital's negligence, complicity, and lack of professionalism appalling. I could easily imagine that doctor as a sexual predator who preyed on heavily sedated female patients. It made me feel sick to my stomach.

From that point on, Dr. Hasegawa became my biggest enemy. Whenever I ran into him in the hallway, I'd shout, "I hate you! Go away, you lecherous pervert! Shoo, shoo!" with a karate kick. He'd pass me quickly with a nervous laugh. This behavior was probably written up too.

But I didn't keep up my rage against Dr. Hasegawa for long. I suspected my hostile behavior was what had landed me in that hospital to begin with, and I feared that if I continued to verbally assault Dr. Hasegawa, they might lock me up for good. Besides, who would take me seriously? I was a seventeen-year-old psychiatric patient. It was too risky to investigate the issue on my own. So, I swallowed my rage and never brought it up again, even though it smoldered inside me.

Then there was another incident. During nighttime rounds I felt a gentle tickling on my pubic area. I opened my eyes and saw a doctor (who now reminds me of a glasses-wearing, beady-eyed Pillsbury Doughboy) staring at me.

"Can you sleep?" he asked.

I gently nodded, closed my eyes, and drifted off.

The next morning when I saw him walking with some other doctors down the hall, I remembered his face and knew he was the one who'd touched me.

"That doctor . . ." I pointed at him, "touched me right here." I then pointed toward my vagina.

Dr. Doughboy had a stern look on his face. "I did not!" he shouted and scurried past. Other staff members ignored me and kept walking.

In sharp contrast to these appalling experiences was the positive interaction I had with a conscientious doctor named Dr. Oki. He was in his mid-thirties, and the top of his head was balding. His eyes were warm and gentle behind his round glasses, and they disappeared when he smiled. He was quick-witted and came across as a scholar. He spoke calmly in a monotone voice that made him sound like a whimsical robot. When I became upset about my declining ability to learn the English vocabulary words listed in my English textbook, he helped me study, turning the memorization into fun quizzes. He continued to check on me even though I wasn't his patient.

I was also appreciative of my many visitors during my two-month stint at the hospital. Considering how far they had to travel, I felt deeply indebted to them. In the beginning my homeroom teacher came, and a few days later, my best friend and classmate Yukiko. Apparently, Mom also came by twice a week or so to drop off my favorite snack foods and fruits, sets of new pajamas, and changes of clothes, but she didn't come to see me. Maybe she was afraid of upsetting me, or my doctors might have warned her not to visit. My sister-in-law Kyoko-san and her mother, who I adoringly called Auntie Ikeda-san, also came. Even Jun-chan came to visit once with his girlfriend. I was thrilled to have these visitors but felt terribly sad after they left.

On February 15, a few days after I became more fully awake and somewhat clearheaded, Dr. Yamaguchi, the ward director, asked me to come to one of the conference rooms after lunch. Not knowing what to expect, I knocked on the door and entered the room. I realized it was a new patient introductory presentation to the medical staff. In other words, an interrogation session. The room was big enough to contain a hundred people, and there were at least fifty attendees, including doctors, interns, medical students, and some nurses. It was a teaching hospital, so everyone had a notepad and pen, ready to record whatever I had to say. Fifty sets of eyes scrutinized me. I felt suffocated.

Dr. Yamaguchi signaled me to sit down in a chair facing him.

"I'm still feeling very tired, so I don't want to talk much." I was curt. "Please make your questions easy and short. I'll only answer yes-no questions."

A moment of silence.

"There's nothing wrong with me, so I don't know why I'm here," I said, pouting. *Mom is the crazy one, not me.*

"You were about to go *kuru-kuru-paa*," Dr. Yamaguchi said, making a cuckoo-circling motion with his finger at the side of his head. "Shige-chan, *kuru-kuru-paa*," he said again in an impish tone of voice, crossing his eyes.

His facial expression and gestures were so comical that I burst out laughing. In hindsight, I should have found his gesticulation grossly inappropriate and offensive. But I thought he was trying to make me laugh so that I'd loosen up and start talking—which was exactly what happened.

I shared the history of my problematic relationship with my mom, how much I despised her for being so selfish and neglectful, how her superstitions instilled unnecessary fear in me, such as when she told me that the spirits of the animals I'd accidentally killed would come back to haunt me, or when my assigned third-grader ID number was #39, and she said it meant "full of suffering."

"Wow, what a memory," one of the interns mumbled.

Then I told them about the American family in Napa and how vastly different they'd been from my Japanese family. I told them I'd already realized how dysfunctional my Japanese family was—Dad was a workaholic, Mom was a narcissist who was never around, and my two brothers were always out doing their own things. Seeing how close the Schmidts were, how they enjoyed each other's company, eating dinner together and sharing conversations, created a painful contrast. Joanne was especially loving and caring, so when I returned home, I suffered a sort of familial culture shock.

"Now I want to ask you something," Dr. Yamaguchi said. "In late January, why did you call Ms. Iida? Remember you called her and thanked her? You were also crying, no?"

"Oh, that. I just wanted to let her know how much I appreciated her kindness and generosity for having taken care of me. She and her family had taken me in when I was three months old and treated me like one of their own."

The interns studied me with intense curiosity—some leaning forward, some whispering while rapidly taking notes.

"My parents took these caretakers for granted," I added, "but not me. Thanking people for their kindness seemed like an obvious, courteous thing to do."

"But everybody worried that you might commit suicide," said Dr. Yamaguchi.

"What an overreaction. Really, there was nothing more to it. It was amusing, though, that soon after that, one by one, my surrogate mothers showed up." I held up a finger for each one. "Yamada-san,

Kimura-san, Matsumoto-san, Kobayashi-san. It was like a caregiver reunion. I had no idea why."

"They were worried about you," Dr. Yamaguchi said. "Do you remember that you locked yourself in your room and stayed up all night for a week, refusing to eat?"

"I really just wanted to figure out life, get to the bottom of the meaning and purpose of life. And I think I attained *satori* in the end."

"Enlightenment is fine," Dr. Yamaguchi said with a chuckle, "but you're better off attaining it when you're healthy."

More scribbling and whispering.

I thought for a moment. "Maybe you're right." In truth, my enlightenment had been kind of half-baked. "If I was truly enlightened, I should have been able to forgive and accept everyone." However, I was mad as hell, especially at my mom, whose wildly inconsistent and contrary behaviors made no sense to me. "My parents have a schizophrenic combination of laissez-faire and overreaction."

At the word "schizophrenic," everybody looked up.

"My mom's a drama queen who goes from one crisis to another," I said, "overreacting all the time. That's why I'm here, right? Not eating and not sleeping?" *Better put her in a mental hospital.* I sighed, slumping down in my chair.

I don't remember how they responded, but I kept talking for probably close to an hour by the time the session ended. There was no follow-up to this big interview, and all I could remember was my discomfort that every staff member knew the details of my life, which made me even more self-conscious. There was no talk therapy; all I was made to do was take meds and rest.

Dr. Yamaguchi, the director of the psych ward, was in his late sixties. He was a small man, very dignified. His short, silver hair was always neatly combed, and his gentle, expressive eyes behind his wire-rimmed glasses were quite charming. He was funny, and I felt relaxed around him. I liked imagining him as Saint Peter guarding the gates of heaven because of our shared beliefs in Christianity and because he had the final say on when I could get out. I still believed in Christianity back then, having attended a Christian school for several years, and had at one point even considered getting baptized. He'd smile whenever he saw me teaching the Lord's Prayer to an elderly patient who I thought of as Old Grandpa, who often came to me complaining of severe headaches.

Keeping my boredom at bay by watching TV or playing ping-pong with wardmates soon grew tiresome. Just getting through each day at the hospital was excruciating, but I was also concerned about the side effects of the variety of pills they made me take. It never occurred to me to ask what the medications were for. Without any knowledge of my diagnosis I periodically harassed Dr. Yamaguchi, asking when I could stop my medications or be released from the hospital.

One day he stopped me with just a few words. "You have a brain disease, so it'll take a while." On another day he said, "You have to be patient. Besides, there's no one at home waiting for you, is there?"

My heart sank. He was right—there was indeed no one anxiously awaiting my return. "My dogs are waiting," I shot back. "I know they miss me."

Within three weeks of my admission, I was transferred from the private room to room 207, a larger room I was to share with five other patients. Much of the time they came across as quite normal, but their symptoms came in waves, and when that happened, they seemed caught up in their own zombie existence. Their faces became stiff and transfixed, eyes haunted with fear or sadness. There was an unspoken rule of etiquette: no one ever mentioned anything about another person's illness. (Though it's possible that, like myself, they didn't even know what was wrong with them.)

Despite that, I found them all very kind and gentle and felt an immediate connection with them. They made me feel accepted and happy. Maybe because I radiated positivity, some doctors and patients (even from other rooms) often stopped by to chat with me.

One of my wardmates spent a long time at the sink, washing her hands over and over. Anyone could tell she was suffering from OCD. A petite, middle-aged schoolteacher, she had a warm, friendly smile that made her cheeks squish up. She always wore the same white pajamas with a red windowpane design, the pants rolled up to her knees. Her bed was kitty-corner from mine, and although I tried not to stare, I couldn't help but notice her repeatedly wiping the inside and outside of her gray steel nightstand. Ironically, despite her fear of germs, she neglected her personal hygiene. She wouldn't bathe, wash her face, or brush her teeth. She came across as nice and approachable, but I was afraid of getting too close because of her bad breath and yellow teeth with food stuck in between.

Then a new patient was moved to our room—a tall, slender, middle-aged woman, very quiet, with no facial expressions. With her shoulder-length hair, porcelain skin, and big brown eyes, I imagined how attractive she would be if she were healthy. But her eyes were lifeless, filled with sadness and despair.

She wore a long, turquoise nightgown with lace trim that made her look elegant. I especially liked her slippers: moss-green and heeled, with a patchwork ribbon in the center. When I asked where she bought them, she muttered, "Takashimaya Department Store." It was the only time I heard her speak. She also refused to eat, so sometimes I went to her side with my room buddy, Naomi, and encouraged her. When I brought her apple slices and offered to feed her, she accepted with a nod and faint smile, and slowly and reluctantly opened her mouth to eat just a few pieces. Naomi and I tried to engage her in conversation, but she remained silent. Even when her husband came to visit her, she hardly spoke. He would leave dispirited. He seemed like a sweet, quiet man. For some reason, he liked me and twice gave me a small box of soft caramels.

About a week into her hospitalization, we were having a business-as-usual kind of day. In the evening we ate dinner facing away from each other with our dinner trays on our own nightstands. As we started eating, I heard what sounded like scraping by the window. When I turned my head, the new patient was climbing over the windowsill. Someone must have opened the window to let in some fresh air. There was a single metal bar across the window, but it was easy enough to climb over.

"Oh *no*!" I screamed as I rushed to the window with the other roommates, but it was too late. A few seconds later, her body, in her turquoise nightgown, slammed against the concrete pavement. She died on impact. As we stood looking down in horror, a few hospital employees dashed out to check on her.

This was the first and only time I'd ever witnessed such a horrific scene. I was dazed and speechless and, like everyone else, couldn't resume eating my dinner. Her husband came by later to collect her belongings. He was obviously distressed but seemed resigned as if he'd been preparing for something like this. Looking down, he kept murmuring, "*Shikata ga nai.* It could not be helped."

Later that evening an elegant bouquet of white orchids was displayed on top of the woman's rolling tray table that hovered over the foot of her bed in view of everyone in the room. Naomi and I both watched as a petal from the orchid drifted onto the table, sending shivers down our spines. We thought maybe her spirit had caused the petal to drop and was still around.

That night we had trouble sleeping. As I lay in bed, staring at the ceiling, I wondered, *If I stay locked up too long, will that happen to me?* Luckily, however, I was released from the hospital a few weeks later.

At the time of my hospital discharge on March 30, 1979, my doctors provided my parents with only a general diagnosis: *shinshinsho* (stress-induced psychosomatic disorder) . . . a nervous breakdown. I wasn't sure whether the diagnosis was vague because they didn't want to reveal the exact nature of my illness or because they simply didn't know. But on the day I was set free, I was too overjoyed to care.

It was late morning when my parents showed up. My dad wore a dark-gray suit and a tie with his ever-present Rotary Club lapel pin. My mom looked immaculate as always in a Jackie Onassis style suit in black-and-white houndstooth, complete with large pearl earrings and her signature magenta-rose lipstick. Her then favorite Chanel perfume, N° 19, was a bit too intense for my liking, but she knew how to make herself look classy and attractive.

I smiled with joy as I told them how excited I was to be released. My dad hugged me, tearing up and saying he was pleased to see me fully recovered and happy again. My mom stroked my back, nodding and smiling as if to second him. We headed over to the nurses' station to give them a box of assorted cookies that my mom had brought as a thank-you gift. My parents then disappeared with Dr. Yamaguchi to his office.

While I waited for them to return, Dr. Asano walked past carrying a box and a couple of bags. I hurried over to help her.

While we walked together to her office, I smiled and said, "Thanks for everything."

She smiled back. In her delicate voice she said, "I'm so glad to know you're such a sweet person after all. I was really concerned about you at the beginning. You were so angry and combative." She paused for a moment, as though debating whether to say more. "You know," she said in a sad, contemplative tone, "given the neglect you've endured your entire life, it's no surprise that you ended up developing those symptoms."

I'd heard similar sentiments from several of the other medical staff. I felt vindicated to know I wasn't so crazy after all. What a remarkable turnaround from having no allies at the beginning of this ordeal. Though I was happy to leave the hospital, I was also a little sad to say goodbye to those who'd stood by my side.

After dropping off Dr. Asano's box in her office, I walked back to my hospital room. Sterile, white walls bordered the long, empty hallway. Old Grandpa shuffled toward me, repeatedly tapping the side of his head—his characteristic gesture signifying an incapacitating pain. I felt sad for him but refrained from approaching to recite the Lord's Prayer with him as I often had. Now that I was leaving, there seemed little I could offer to help him. He would be on his own. I went back to sit on my bed and wait for my parents.

When they returned from Dr. Yamaguchi's office, my mom stomped into the room, red-faced, clenching her teeth. "How rude and insulting!" she said to my dad. "Who does he think he is to tell us how to raise our daughter?" She turned to me. "He glared at us like this . . ." She leaned toward me, scowling, shaking her head, and jabbing her finger in the air. "And then said, 'Shame on you for treating your daughter this way. It's totally unacceptable.'"

Dr. Yamaguchi had drawn this conclusion based on the report from my team of doctors who'd conducted in-depth interviews with every visitor who'd come to see me in the hospital—family members, family friends, friends, teachers, and acquaintances.

My mom's impersonation of Dr. Yamaguchi looked so funny, like a parent scolding a misbehaving child, that I chuckled and brushed it off as unimportant. Once again, though, I felt vindicated. It was heartwarming to know that Dr. Yamaguchi, a man of few words, cared enough about me to rebuke my parents.

My dad looked down, speechless. What was he feeling? Ashamed? Humiliated? Embarrassed? Had his image of the perfect family come crumbling down? Had the image of himself he'd worked so hard to achieve—tireless surgeon, owner and director of his hospital, a well-recognized and respected philanthropist in the community who'd devoted decades to the Boy Scouts and Rotary Club—been debunked? He looked so dejected that I didn't dare to ask. After abdicating his family responsibilities for so long, he seemed at a loss for what to do with the family anymore. Together with my clueless and equally uninvolved mom, I wasn't too optimistic that things at home would improve.

My family *did* follow the doctors' post-discharge treatment plan—which involved me staying on my meds and all of us spending more time together—at least for a little while.

One evening, the whole family sat down at the kitchen table to cook meat and vegetables on the portable tabletop grill for dinner. Mom was hustling to transfer bell peppers and onions onto the grill when she accidentally knocked over the soy sauce bottle and freaked out. While she blotted the spill, just to piss her off, I stuck my chopsticks vertically into my bowl of rice—a symbol of death.

"Oh no, that's bad luck." She yanked the chopsticks out and laid them down on the table. Everyone focused on the cooking to avoid eye contact. There seemed to be nothing to talk about, so I broached some safe discussion topics, like how eating vegetables was good for one's health and when the rain might return. The whole thing was so unnatural that I could sense their discomfort, not knowing what to say to each other.

These dinners were short-lived. As soon as I appeared to be back to normal, they returned to their comfort zone of *barabara* (separate/disconnected) again.

Years later when I became curious about my illness and asked my mom about it, the only thing she could recall was that it was an illness of "entitled, spoiled children." I was dismayed to find that her interpretation had missed the important take-home message that Dr. Yamaguchi and Dr. Asano had pointed out on my discharge day: my illness was rooted in family dysfunction and parental neglect.

After the hospital discharge, I went back to school but was so sedated and incapacitated by the side effects of the psychiatric drugs—extreme drowsiness and fatigue, dizziness, blurred vision, an inability to focus, memory loss, worsening depression and anxiety, and even occasional suicidal thoughts—that I could barely function. To top it off, I'd developed severe acne and constipation. The combination of these symptoms not only severely hindered my progress to get healthy but also made it impossible for me to function at school. I was scared that I might be losing my mind. I cried over the phone and during biweekly outpatient visits, pleading with my doctors to stop or at least reduce the dosage of the medications. They claimed that either option had to be done in the hospital, where they could monitor me 24/7.

So, within a couple of months, I readmitted myself to the same psych ward voluntarily. It was a true testimony to my degree of desperation. The three extremely cautious doctors in charge of my care put me through a painstaking, oh-so-slow process of reducing the dosages of my medication one by one. It took nearly three months and was such a frustrating and mind-numbing ordeal—disheartening enough to make me wonder if my messed-up brain would ever be normal again.

The No-Nonsense Family Counselor

December 2013 to May 2014

Between the trip to France, my continuing parenting battles with Peter, and the morning hell incident where David threatened to jump from the moving car, I decided it was time to make an appointment with a family counselor. Janice, an expert in parenting teenagers, came highly recommended. Unfortunately, there was a wait of several weeks.

In the meantime, David's romance with Liz had intensified. Convinced they were soulmates, they made up for their weekday long-distance relationship by spending every minute of their weekends together through sleepovers, either at our house in Seattle or hers in Bellingham. Peter and I were clueless about how to set sensible limits and enforce them, and had inadvertently allowed the two teens to take the driver's seat.

One Saturday afternoon in early December, David waltzed into the kitchen and said, "Mom, will you take me to the Amtrak station in half an hour?"

"No." I was in the middle of cleaning out the fridge, surrounded by condiments. "I can't just drop everything and take you there. You spent the last two weekends with her family. You need to spend time with your friends here, too, or you'll be alienated at school."

"I don't care about that," he said. "I just want to be with Liz."

We went back and forth for a while until I eventually gave up and gave in. It just seemed easier. Many weekends went like this. My efforts to tap the brakes on their relationship by setting arbitrary limits only backfired and ended in shouting matches. Peter didn't help much (or didn't know how) to reduce the tension in the house, dismissing my concerns as an overreaction.

And then, one late afternoon, Liz showed up at our front door after driving ninety miles from Bellingham because she was having a "crisis."

The counseling sessions couldn't start soon enough.

Our initial ninety-minute session was scheduled for the first Thursday in December 2013. Peter, David, and I sat silently in the waiting room, tense and anxious. As David stared at his iPhone, Peter flipped through an old copy of *TIME Magazine*, and I examined some Japanese artifacts on the wall. Janice had a short haircut and wore no makeup, which made her face look stern. From the way she greeted us in a deep, flat voice with business-like manners, I instantly sensed she was not the touchy-feely type.

It was late afternoon. The sun was already setting, and the faint evening light came through the window as we settled into her office. Though it was slightly cluttered, the built-in bookshelves filled with books and knickknacks gave the room a cozy atmosphere. A miniature stained-glass tree of life sat on the coffee table next to the window, filtering the light. I loved the tree of life artwork and its spiritual meaning: the interconnectedness of everything, growth and strength, individuality, and peace. I had a larger version of it propped against a living room window in our house.

David sat in the ivory love seat to the right of the counselor's chair, I sank into the comfy, beige armchair directly facing her, and Peter sat in the brown leather armchair on her left. The atmosphere was heavy and tense.

"So, what brought you guys here?" Janice asked.

I perceived this as an invitation to unload all the anger, frustration, and fear that had been festering for months. Talk therapy was my kind of thing, and I was a seasoned client, although I'd been making do without it lately, as I hadn't found a therapist who worked well with me. I dove right in and soon dominated the conversation with the long list of complaints I had about David, from his morning madness, explosive tantrums, poor time management, and chronic sleep deprivation caused by the long Skype sessions with Liz on school nights, to his self-imposed social isolation at school.

Janice interjected. "What's the biggest fear you have for him?" She got straight to the point, I'd give her that.

I mulled over her question. "That he won't realize his full potential."

Peter nodded as if to second what I'd said. David kept mum.

"Are you afraid the relationship with Liz might sabotage his potential?" Janice asked.

"Well . . . yeah, sort of. I do have misgivings about it. It seems so emotionally intense, obsessive, and codependent. I'm also worried about how her depressive personality might affect David. But what can I say? I'm a worrywart. Oh, and her mother, Diane." I sighed deeply. "She's an absolute nightmare—way too involved in facilitating that relationship." My opinion of Diane had changed drastically since the lunch we'd had at Monkey Bridge.

David, lips pursed and fists clenched, was barely managing to keep his temper in check. A fidgeter by nature, he looked like he was sitting on an anthill.

I talked about Liz's emotional fragility and depression—for which she'd been taking medication since before she'd met David. Seeing her depressive tendencies was like reliving my own teenage traumas, and it was unbearably painful. Every time I overheard her say on Skype, "It was the worst day of my life," I flinched.

I described an occurrence one past weekday evening when David was bombarded with a heavy load of homework. Liz had called from her doctor's office in Seattle, saying she had to see him.

"I was so tired of her repeated crises, I totally lost it and couldn't stand seeing her. So I jumped in the car with our dog and fled to the drugstore just to hang out. I stayed there until David called to let me know she'd left."

"I didn't know you did that," Peter said, catching himself slouching and immediately straightening his posture.

I shrugged. "I've been trying to make sense of what's been happening for a long time now." It was tempting to put all the blame on Diane, but I knew I couldn't do that. "It's partially my fault that I didn't speak up early to agree on appropriate boundaries. It's just that I didn't expect to keep dealing with unreasonable demands."

As a member of the Seattle Youth Symphony Orchestra, Liz had to come all the way to Seattle from Bellingham on most Saturday mornings for rehearsal. For the first few weeks, I didn't mind driving David to her rehearsals for their Saturday afternoon rendezvous, but that soon extended to her coming over to our house after each rehearsal. Then their weekly dates came to involve Liz staying overnight at our house on Friday (and sometimes also Saturday) nights.

When I objected to Liz's frequent visits, saying they were an encroachment on our family space, David started spending the rest of the weekend with her family. They would go back to Bellingham together by train or bus after her rehearsal, with David then returning on the late Sunday night Amtrak. All the while, either Peter or I served as chauffeurs to facilitate their whims and desires, shuttling back and forth between our home and the downtown Greyhound station or the Edmonds Amtrak station in a "Your wish is our command, Prince David and Princess Liz" kind of way. Looking back, Peter and I should have put a stop to this early on, but since Peter was okay with it, I grudgingly went along without thinking about the repercussions. I supposed I was also just too tired to stand my ground.

David picked at his hangnails, looking furious, but I pretended not to notice. I told Janice that perhaps my Japanese aversion to confrontation and my difficulty saying no were at least partly to blame.

"But what irks me even more," I said, raising my voice, "is that throughout all these complicated arrangements and hassles, there hasn't been even a single email or phone call from Liz's family to give us any heads-up or ask if it was okay with us."

After voicing my thoughts about Liz's mother's brazenness, I gave Janice an unsolicited cultural lesson: In Japan, imposing on others is called *zuzushii* (being shamelessly brazen), a social faux pas to avoid at all costs.

"If someone ever called me *zuzushii*, I'd feel so embarrassed and ashamed," I said.

"I'm not Japanese," Janice said, "but I find it offensive and intrusive too."

"Several of my American friends also think it's an infringement,"

I said. "Liz's family is taking advantage of us since our house serves as such a convenient way station to get to SYSO rehearsals. But Peter doesn't see it that way." I glanced at him, feeling buoyed by the safe environment to speak my mind. "I've been feeling so alone in this, wondering if I'm too narrow-minded. Peter goes to the other extreme though. Love thy neighbor, even though he's an atheist."

"I hear you," Janice said.

"But David is the driving force in all this. He's always been challenging for me, but this is a different kind of challenge—so contrary, contentious, and defiant—and he twists everything into an argument. Sometimes I can barely tolerate his obnoxious behavior, which only feeds into my menopausal temper."

"But he's a teenager," Janice said. "That's how teenagers behave." She turned to Peter. "Why do you think Shigeko takes things so personally?"

He took off his glasses and rubbed his eyes. "I don't know."

"Because David really pisses me off," I said, even though it didn't really answer her question.

"But you're the adult," Janice said.

Her comment took me aback. "Just recently, I became so angry and fed up that I threw a tantrum and said, 'You don't seem to care what I think. So do whatever you want. I don't care anymore!'" A tantrum. But I was the adult. I shifted in my chair.

Janice turned to David. "How did that make you feel?"

David remained silent.

"You don't like to hear what she just said, do you?"

Scowling and pursing his lips, he still kept mum.

She looked at Peter and me. "See what's happening here?" She turned to David. "You feel hurt, don't you? Why don't you tell your mom how you feel?"

"I . . ." David stopped and took a long, strained breath. "I don't want to."

"Why not?" Janice pressed.

He looked away, trying to hide his welling eyes. "Because . . . " His voice quivered. "I don't want Mom to know . . . she has power over me." Then he started to cry.

I felt a rush of hurt. "Oh, but I don't matter in this family, so whatever I say shouldn't make any difference."

"Come on," Janice said, "you're his mother. You've been heavily involved in his life. He's so dependent on you. And *you* also say a lot. You really do. Sometimes it's better to keep your mouth shut." She zipped a hand across her lips.

I felt ashamed, remembering the lunch at Monkey Bridge at which I'd spoken way too much.

"You put yourself in that position!" Peter said, his voice rising. "You know, that reminds me. Back when David was seven, he spilled some milk inside the refrigerator, and she got really mad and said, 'I'm not going to be your mother anymore. I'm going to go back to Japan and leave you here.' It was the only time she said something like that, but it was so shocking that I wrote it down."

I had said it. It was something I'd wanted to forget. *I was just having a temper tantrum. I really didn't mean it*, I felt like shouting, but I felt too sheepish to say anything. I was mortified to realize that I was making the same mistakes my mother had made, displaying the same callous behavior I despised so much and swore I'd never repeat. It was the one thing I'd wanted to do—spare David from the loneliness and emptiness I'd felt growing up with my emotionally hollow and disconnected family in Japan—and I had failed.

"You *are* powerful, even though you may not know it," Janice said.

"That's why those little things you say have such a big impact. Don't do that. It's very destructive."

My feelings of shame and guilt culminated at that moment. Blood rushed to my head, and I felt dizzy. My body tensed up, and the pain in my neck and lower back intensified. I rearranged the pillows behind me and kept shifting to find more comfort. At the same time, I found it strangely reassuring to have an authority figure who cared enough about us to point out so clearly and poignantly what I was doing wrong.

I also hadn't realized until that moment how toxic my age-old habit of discounting my self-worth had been to our family, as well as how my empty threat to leave the family (just like my mother had threatened) had eroded Peter's trust in me and was eating away at our marriage.

"Back to the issue of David and Liz," Janice said. "How long has it been since this whole thing started?"

"A little more than three months," I said.

"Then it's not too late to change," she said. "But you'd better put your foot down now. The longer you wait, the harder it'll be."

We crammed a lot into the session and managed to come up with a rough framework of limits for David, with the overall goal of reducing the amount of yelling in the house. Though the details (such as Skype privileges and frequency of sleepovers) still had to be worked out in the coming sessions, Janice spelled out some basic limits for David:

- Keep up the good schoolwork.
- Keep up with friendships at school.
- Get decent sleep.
- Don't become Liz's emotional crutch.

That was how our first crash course in parenting ended. We agreed to meet again at the same time each week for the foreseeable future.

When we stepped out of the office, no one spoke. The limit setting didn't sit well with David. He was visibly upset, so angry with me that he rode home with Peter, and I drove home alone.

It was me versus them. Again.

But just because we knew what to do didn't mean it was easy to do it.

In another session, Janice began by asking us, "How are things going?"

The answer was, "Not so well."

We were now paying the price for our permissive parenting—coddling, overindulging, catering to David's whims, and setting no boundaries. Given the way I'd been raised, I didn't have much confidence in my parenting skills, especially with a teenager, so I turned to Peter who'd had a more normal upbringing. Yet I found myself disappointed and discouraged each time he disputed or dismissed my instinct to say no and set limits. He called it arbitrary, overstepping, and meddling.

"I think Peter is way too lenient," I said. "Maybe because he grew up with a strict father. So he says yes to almost everything. If David comes to me first and I say no, he pushes and pushes, yells, and throws a tantrum until I get so exhausted, I give in." I gathered my courage despite the tightness in my chest. "He just doesn't take no for an answer. I'm so tired of bearing the brunt of his anger when I'm trying to restore some kind of order in the house."

"Of course he's going to push," Janice said. "He's a teenager. It's your job to be stronger and not give in."

Sure. I wished I had that kind of strength.

A good half of the session was spent reaffirming our lack of parenting skills. Janice kept calling us out whenever we told her how we often dealt with situations, which was by leaving David to his own devices.

"That's not parenting," she'd say in that tough-love voice, shaking her head, incredulous.

All the while we sat there frozen, feeling small and intimidated as if an overbearing teacher was scolding us.

At one point, apparently losing her patience, she said brusquely, "Do you want me to teach you how to parent?"

We both nodded.

"You don't ask him to do something. You *tell* him!"

It was so obvious, I couldn't believe we hadn't thought of it. Peter seemed a bit taken aback. We then discussed how to help David improve his time management skills.

"Sounds like he needs a study coach," Janice said.

"Well, if he needs one, he can search the internet and find someone himself," Peter said.

"No! That's *your* job," she snapped. "You're treating him like an adult."

"Yeah." David's voice quivered. "They've been so hands-off and not at all helpful, so I've been struggling all by myself."

It touched a nerve. *Oh my god, that's exactly what I had to do as a child.* "I'll contact his school counselor and get a referral from her," I said.

Even after all the admonishments about our parenting (or lack thereof), I didn't shy away from exposing our mistakes. I couldn't help myself.

One Sunday in November, when David had returned from another weekend "adoption" in Bellingham, I was obsessively sweeping pine needles off the front hallway.

"Hi, David," I said rather flatly and went right back to the chore.

"We are a bad family," he yelled. "I hate living in this house!" Then he stormed to his room and slammed the door.

What the hell? I stood there dazed.

Peter was the one who had picked him up at the Edmonds Amtrak station and driven him home. When he walked in from the garage, I asked him what had happened. "Didn't he have a good time with Liz's family?"

"Nothing happened," he said. "David said he had a great time. They went to a pumpkin patch, made cookies, and went to a local craft shop to do some art activities."

Aha. After having so much fun and being treated as if he were a knight in shining armor, coming home must have felt like a letdown. And when I hadn't greeted him with a hug and a heartfelt, "Welcome home! I missed you!" the way Diane did, he'd snapped. A lot like how I felt and behaved when I came home to my cold, absent family in Japan after having had a wonderful time with my Napa host family.

At our following counseling session, I said to Janice, "David often comments on how Diane is deeply engaged in her daughters' lives and that she likes doing art projects with them. I wish I had that kind of energy, but I don't. So I don't blame him." For a moment, I felt bad about my general lack of enthusiasm for life. But that didn't stop me from sharing another episode: a ridiculously over-the-top

Tolo/turnabout dance proposal for which David decided to defy its tradition of girls asking boys to the dance.

It was already past midnight. David still had lots of homework to finish, but he was trying to make big letters—LIZ TOLO?—out of cardboard. Poor at time management and planning ahead as usual, he had waited until the last minute and was freaking out. It made no sense to me. Why make such a big deal for a sophomore high school dance? But he was determined to get it done.

Peter, who loved art projects, took over this task with gusto, cutting out the letters, wrapping them with aluminum foil, and securing them with Scotch tape. Despite my frustration with David, I felt obligated to participate, so I joined in, decorating each letter with turquoise glitter. In the midst of this project, David said with delight, "Look, Mom. We're doing a family project."

Yeah right, an annoying midnight project you should have done by yourself.

He planned to display these letters on a restaurant table at the foot of the Seattle Great Wheel so that once he and Liz reached the top, he could say, "Hey, Liz, look down there!" If things went off without a hitch, Liz would be very moved, hug him, and say yes. David had originally planned to involve his friends, having them stand at the base of the Ferris wheel and hold up the letters. But I adamantly opposed making the whole thing so complicated. Instead, Peter and I ended up getting involved.

The next evening, we took David and Liz to the Ferris wheel, and while they waited to board, we dashed three blocks back to our car to retrieve those giant silver letters from the trunk, then rushed back to the adjacent restaurant where David had prearranged to use their patio table to display the letters. We spoke with the hostess who thought we were helping to prepare for a surprise marriage proposal (in fact, the restaurant was a popular site for that very thing), and she seemed dumbfounded that it was just a high school dance invitation. She led us to the patio, and a waiter helped us arrange the tables to display the letters. We then sat inside the restaurant and waited for the two lovebirds. Peter enjoyed a beer and seemed unfazed by this elaborate operation. I remained dazed and flummoxed. I felt the dramatic invitation was ridiculous and wondered why we'd gotten involved. I didn't even want to imagine what his marriage proposal would look like.

In the end, David's plan was a huge success. Liz was touched and happy, and he was proud to have pulled off such a feat. Peter seemed satisfied that it had worked out. I, on the other hand, was disgruntled and apathetic about having been dragged into it but kept those unpleasant feelings to myself. After that, every speck of turquoise glitter that I spotted in our house or garage was like smoldering tinder, instantly reigniting my anger.

"I really hate to feel this way," I said to Janice. "It makes me feel like a bitchy ogre."

"Why don't you just let him fail?" she asked. "You guys didn't have to do all the work for him. If you keep bailing him out, he won't learn. All you have to say is no. Why is it so hard for you to say no to him?"

Inside, I was seething at what felt like judgment. "Oh, I don't know. Maybe I'm afraid of his explosive temper that goes from zero to sixty, his glare, his gritting teeth."

"But he's a teenager," she said. "You have to put your foot down."

No doubt she was right about that. But saying it was one thing. I had no idea how to do it.

Inspired by our sessions with Janice, I mustered my courage to call Diane and enlist her help in limiting David and Liz's Skype usage on school nights so that David could have a decent night's sleep. Diane apparently didn't set any limits. The only one I knew of was that David and Liz slept in separate bedrooms when they had sleepovers, and whenever they were in the same room, the door had to stay open.

But instead of suggesting something constructive, Diane said, "You do know how lonely David is, right? He needs more connection at home."

She might have meant well, but I felt chagrined, and then furious. After hanging up the phone I dashed down to David's room and shouted, "How dare you tell them you're lonely and needing connection. I've been there for you every step of the way, no matter what, but you take everything I do for granted."

David looked up from his desk, startled.

"I'm sorry I haven't been as good a mom as you want me to be," I said, with angry tears in my eyes.

He stood up and came over to me. "You *are* a good mother, in fact, a great mother. You're just not a good mom."

"What's the difference?"

"You do things out of parental obligation."

Bam! I felt like I'd been hit by a brick. *And wow, how perceptive.* There were days when I found myself barely tolerating his behavior, and he had seen right through me. On those days, I'd daydream about how peaceful my life would be when he left for college, and then I'd feel guilty.

I remembered the times when we had built his favorite Lego Bionicle with so much joy and excitement. The times he'd put out pots and pans on the kitchen floor and strike them with a wooden spoon, smiling and giggling as he made his own music. His cute little voice singing the theme song to *Olive, the Other Reindeer.* Those times it was so easy to love him no matter how much of a handful he was. But even then, my constant worries and anxiety over his health and well-being prevented me from being truly in the moment. And as my life grew lethargic and joyless, I lost my sense of humor and rarely smiled or laughed.

He pressed on. "Mom, you have a PhD from Stanford. Why aren't you using it? Is it all because of me?"

At first, I was so stunned that I didn't know what to say. He was partially right. But I said, "No, of course not. It was because of the circumstances. It was hard to get back into academia, that's all. Don't ever think it was your fault."

I did, in fact, try to get back into academia after a long hiatus. I worked as a research assistant for a professor at the University of Washington School of Nursing and cowrote a chapter with her for a resource guide called *Transcultural Aspects of Perinatal Health Care.* But that job ended after she lost a tenure fight. When I couldn't land another research position, I gave up. Looking back, I might have been suffering from low-grade depression; I became so easily discouraged and unmotivated.

I felt like a total failure all over again. I'd sacrificed and worked so hard to spare David the fate of loneliness I'd suffered myself. I broke down and cried, and David hugged me and started to sob.

"I'm sorry, Mom," he said. "I didn't really mean it. I just wanted to get your attention."

Peter heard us and came down from the kitchen to check on us. When he saw us hugging, he wrapped his long arms around us and joined in.

Then there was the session when Peter and I showed up without David, who had an unexpected scheduling conflict. I assumed we'd talk more about our parenting problems and celebrate our recent successes, but Janice had something else in mind.

"How are you two guys doing?"

"Not as close as I'd like us to be," Peter said and then started complaining about our lack of sex.

Here we go again. It was an uncomfortable topic I wanted to pretend didn't exist.

"How often do you guys have sex?" Janice asked.

"Um, maybe once a week," I said.

Peter shook his head.

"Once a month?" I suggested.

"Not even close. Three times a year." Peter took off his glasses and rubbed at the bridge of his nose, exasperated.

Janice looked startled.

"I guess, if you don't count blowjobs." I gave a nonchalant shrug.

"I'm talking about intercourse," Peter said, "and it's not at all romantic when she says things like, 'Just concentrate and hurry up.'"

"Do you know how important sex is in a marriage?" Janice said.

Yeah, right, like I've never heard that before. Irritated, I looked away. "Sex isn't all that important to me. It's more like an obligation."

"This has been our major problem ever since David was born," Peter said.

"You know, I usually don't share my personal life with clients," Janice said calmly, yet firmly, "but my husband passed away two years ago, and I really miss our physical contact. That's so important, and you guys are flushing it down the toilet." She turned to me. "Here you have someone who desires you and seeks physical intimacy, and you're pushing him away."

It was a blow to my fragile ego. How could she say that without knowing the underlying issues? I felt like I had to defend myself. I'd been feeling paralyzed by a whole host of issues—insomnia, body aches, postpartum depression, anxiety, PTSD, menopause.

"It all goes back to Peter's inability to empathize," I said, "particularly with my emotional struggles. He thinks being emotional is a sign of weakness. His stoic just-suck-it-up-and-move-on approach feels like a gut punch. It's so dismissive and invalidating." I choked up. "I think my chronic pain became exacerbated by the emotional pain of loneliness and isolation in our marriage. I got so used to repressing my sadness, anger, and resentment that I became numb."

I exhaled deeply and continued. "So yes, we basically drifted apart because when I didn't feel emotionally close, being physically intimate was the last thing on my mind." I said this as if it were a thing of the past. "Once I stopped expecting his emotional support, things became easier for me."

If Peter winced, I didn't notice. I just kept talking. "I took care of myself by turning to writing or talking to my friends or a therapist. I also used alternative medicine, physical therapy, and a sleep disorder doctor to manage my pain and insomnia, and I'm doing much better. We were on the verge of divorce about ten years ago, but we're fine now. We're just going through a rough patch at the moment because of David."

"Oh, but that is *so* sad." Janice's dark eyes were full of sympathy.

Peter kept his gaze focused on the carpet.

I was too mired in my own struggles to notice that our marriage was on life support. I just gave her a what-else-am-I-supposed-to-do look and did what I'd always done: blamed Peter.

Triumphant Return

1993 to 1997

After Joanne showed me around the beautiful Stanford campus while I was staying in Napa, I imagined how nice it would be to study there. Even more, I came to perceive my affiliation with the school as a prerequisite to being fully accepted into the Napa family clan. So, it's not an overstatement to say that the Schmidt family was the sole reason behind my obsession to someday graduate from Stanford myself.

It was July 1983, six years after my initial time with the Schmidts, when I returned to California for a long-term stay. Though I'd wanted to come back sooner, so much had gotten in the way and delayed me—including my stay in the hospital. I told my parents I wanted to go to California to study and brush up on my English skills. I transferred from a small women's college in Tokyo to another small private college in northern California, close enough to visit my host family in Napa.

In truth, all I wanted was to get the hell out of Japan and live near the Schmidts. I didn't have any ambitions beyond that. But as time went by, I came to enjoy studying, especially learning about early childhood development and education, and I wanted to continue—which was a big surprise for someone who'd hated school all her life.

After graduating with a BA, I found temporary employment at a preschool affiliated with Stanford. As luck would have it, the director liked me so much that she sponsored me to obtain an H-1 work visa. I went on to study Montessori education and earned a master's degree. I volunteered for some Stanford research projects and became well enough acquainted with some professors for them to write me letters of recommendation. After all this was done, I finally applied to Stanford. Not long after, I went to pray at Stanford Memorial Church and saw a thick notebook with blank pages lying open on a lectern. It might have been a guest book, but I thought it was a prayer requests book, so I wrote down my prayer to be accepted to my dream school. At any rate, all my efforts plus the prayer must have helped because I was accepted to the PhD program at Stanford's School of Education.

I started to live my dream, and a few years later met the love of my life, Peter.

Peter and I met on Valentine's Day in 1993 when my matchmaker Swedish friend and her roommate hosted a Swedish tea party for singles. With a plethora of decadent sweets, it was a feast for sugar addicts like Peter and me. As I went back for seconds and thirds, Peter did the same, and we laughed and struck up a conversation. We were both in graduate school at Stanford. When I learned he was a Harvard student finishing his research in a Stanford laboratory, my credential-obsessed Japanese self was doubly smitten. We were soon deeply engaged in a discussion about Japanese culture as he eagerly shared his "expert" knowledge from reading a series of San Jose's *Mercury News* articles. We had fun talking and exchanged phone numbers at the end.

Over the following two months, we went out to movies and dinners, and I really liked him but didn't feel like rushing into a new relationship, so I maintained my reserve. The year before, I'd had a difficult breakup and was still not completely healed. I was just beginning to feel comfortable being alone and enjoying life again. Besides, he was moving to Minnesota to attend medical school in the fall, and I wasn't interested in a short-term relationship. But he wasn't willing to give up on me.

On Easter morning, I opened my front door and found an Easter basket elaborately decorated with pink miniature carnations. Inside were all kinds of candies and goodies, along with a white plush rabbit with floppy ears that I later named Peter Rabbit because of its remarkable resemblance to Peter. He had also attached a miniature, handwoven paper basket he'd made for my dog, Shelly, and had filled it with her favorite baby carrots. That was when he won my heart. I felt so happy and loved. I'd never received such a thoughtful Easter basket in my life. Soon we began dating in earnest, though we were unsure of what the future would hold for us.

When Peter drove across the country to move to Minnesota, I came along for the road trip. A few days later, he drove me to the Minneapolis airport for my flight back to San Francisco and we said goodbye, both of us crying so hard that many passersby stared. That was when we realized how attached we were to each other and decided to give our long-distance relationship a chance. We managed to keep it up by writing and occasionally calling, even while I was in Japan to collect data for my dissertation. Shortly after I returned from Japan, he flew out to see me in Palo Alto. It was Valentine's Day

1994, and while sitting on the love seat tenderly kissing, Peter got up and pulled the coffee table to one side. He then got down on one knee, took my hand, and asked me to marry him. In tears, I said yes and hugged him. Later, when we went for a walk around the neighborhood, Peter wove a leaf into a temporary engagement ring and slid it onto my finger.

In mid-September 1994, Peter flew out again to help me drive across the country to Rochester, Minnesota. It wasn't an easy decision for me. I had enjoyed every minute of living in Palo Alto, and I didn't want to move away from the Schmidts. But I was in love with Peter, and we were engaged, so I knew it was the right decision. I'd completed all the requirements for my doctorate as well as three months of fieldwork data collection. All I had left to do was analyze the data and write up the dissertation, which I thought I could easily do remotely.

I married Peter on Valentine's Day 1995. Our wedding was a simple courthouse ceremony and a reception lunch. We mailed out wedding announcements, but mostly without invitations. As much as I wanted my Napa family to be there, I thought it would be too much of an imposition on them, so we invited only Peter's relatives and a handful of friends from the Rochester and Minneapolis areas. My friend Edith, Peter's classmate's wife, became a good friend and was my maid of honor. The wedding, held on a frigid day in Minnesota, was a very small private affair, partly because I was on a tight budget. My Japanese family had been plagued with hideous financial troubles (due to their own mismanagement and aggravated by the burst of Japan's housing bubble). It seemed unfair since Jun-chan's wedding five years earlier had been a jaw-dropping, Hollywood-style event.

But the heartfelt letter my father sent to be read during the reception helped me get over my bitterness. Edith choked up while reading his letter saying how much he missed me and how proud he was of the person I'd become, noting in particular my empathetic, sincere, and sensible nature. Though I tried to remain stoic, I teared up too.

Living in Minnesota was quite interesting from an anthropological perspective. The Californians I'd met seemed open-minded and free-spirited, whereas Minnesotans seemed more reserved and slower to warm up to newcomers. I admired their strong work ethic, sincerity, discipline, and perseverance, which resembled my Japanese culture.

But living there day-to-day was a different story, and my cultural curiosity was soon replaced by loneliness and a sense of dread. I had to tackle my dissertation alone, away from my cohort and thesis advisors, which proved more challenging than I'd expected. It was difficult to keep my motivation alive. It felt like I was leading a monastic life and having to endure three brutal Minnesota winters to boot. I missed living in California and pined for my friends and host family in Napa. I often felt like reaching out to Joanne but didn't want to seem too needy or constantly in survival mode. My phone calls to her became sparse, and when I did call, I kept our conversations light and brief.

A silver lining was that soon after moving to Rochester, I met Edith, who was also working on her doctoral thesis. She'd been to Japan, spoke Japanese, and had an affinity to my culture. We had so much in common, both facing the daunting task of thesis writing with no support net while our spouses were busy with medical school. We became each other's lifelines, both of us feeling so isolated and suffering from cabin fever, especially in the dead of winter when we were snowed in, iced in, and cut off from the rest of the world.

Although there was a support group for spouses of medical students and residents, we felt like misfits and decided not to join. Instead, we got together weekly at the coffee shop inside Barnes & Noble to check in on each other's progress but usually ended up spending much of our time commiserating and bitching about our theses and being stuck in Rochester.

Apart from the time I spent with Edith, my days looked exactly the same. Peter left for medical school while it was still dark outside, so I always woke up alone, feeling heavy and overwhelmed by the work I faced transcribing and analyzing interviews. I made coffee and went through my morning routine. I brushed my teeth but didn't bother washing my face or changing into daywear anymore. Peter's sister had given me a tie-dyed jumpsuit—the only brightly colored item in the gloomy apartment or in the equally gloomy subzero weather outside. I lived in it 24/7. The only time I went outside was to take care of Shelly's potty routine. I got bundled up in heavy winter gear so that she could dash out into the snow, do her business, and dash right back into the apartment.

After breakfast, I wasn't motivated at all to start working. Hours passed with me being unproductive and daydreaming about being back in California. Then it was time for *Days of Our Lives*. I always felt a bit down when it was over.

As soon as I saw the mail truck in the parking lot, I'd rush downstairs to retrieve my mail and chat with our friendly mailman who saw me in the same jumpsuit every day. I was psyched to interact with a human and rambled while he sorted the mail.

Shelly was with me for the first fifteen months I lived in Rochester and always kept me company, staying right beside my feet as I worked deep into the night. But one day in March 1996, she collapsed and passed away shortly after we rushed her to the vet. She was eleven years old. I was devastated and cried on and off for days. Losing her left a gaping hole in my heart, and I felt tremendous guilt thinking that maybe not taking her out on regular walks—something she had loved to do—had precipitated her death. Peter grieved with me, which helped me feel less alone. He thought a change of scenery might help, so we took a weekend trip to the Twin Cities to spend time with his siblings.

Once I'd done enough crying, I thought, *This is it. I'm going to have a baby.* Peter agreed it was time for us to start a family. But all too soon, our sex life became mechanical. I was fiercely determined to get pregnant, recording my temperature and keeping an ovulation chart, lifting my pelvis up in the air for fifteen minutes after intercourse to ensure that the sperm and egg met each month. Frustrated and increasingly impatient after several months of trying, I even had testing done at the Mayo Clinic to see if there was any blockage in my fallopian tubes. The memory of that painful procedure still makes me cringe.

In the meantime, I continued working on my thesis. By the time I finished and was ready to defend it, I was ten weeks pregnant.

It was a cold day in early January 1997, with temperatures hovering in the teens, when I flew from Minnesota to California to defend my doctoral thesis at Stanford. During the four-hour flight, I recalled the long, arduous, thesis journey. This was a huge accomplishment—or it would be if I succeeded. My fear of the oral defense so dwarfed my usual fear of flying that I hardly noticed any turbulence.

Peter had helped me prepare and practice my presentation. I rehearsed using an overhead projector with him as my audience. He'd gone through this process two years earlier, so his tips on making eye contact, pausing occasionally, and speaking more slowly were helpful. But it was my idea to kick off with a five-panel *Dilbert* comic strip that summarized one of my major findings in the simplest way possible. I hoped opening this way might soften the atmosphere and facilitate my presentation.

Shortly before landing, I spotted the magnificent Stanford campus, with its red tile roofs and Spanish colonial buildings. It was like seeing an old friend. I missed this campus so much that it frequently showed up in my dreams. I saw green grass, palms, and eucalyptus trees instead of snow, icicles, and bare trees. It had been only a little over two years since I'd left, but it seemed like a decade.

While I was glued to the aerial view of the Quad and Memorial Church, where I'd once prayed to be accepted as a student, I remembered how much I'd loved living in my quaint studio cottage apartment. Hummingbirds had been frequent visitors to my feeder outside the tiny kitchen window. I had so enjoyed taking daily and nightly walks with my beloved Shelly around the neighborhood. Shelly had radiated happiness with her whole body and made everyone she encountered smile and want to pet her.

As I headed over to the rental car counter, I basked in the bright sunshine and mild temperature—probably forty to fifty degrees warmer than where I'd been just four hours earlier.

I had planned a four-day trip, where I would stay at Joanne and Richard's house in Napa for the first night before heading to Palo Alto for two nights. As I arrived at their house, I exhaled a deep sigh of relief at the reassuringly familiar sight, the place where my dreams of America had all begun. When Joanne and Richard came out to greet me, I was almost in tears.

Over dinner, Richard and I exchanged our usual good-natured

banter. I also shared my impressions of living in the Midwest and my difficulty adjusting.

"Well, you've been spoiled from living in some of the best places in America," Richard said. "Napa, Mendocino, San Francisco, and Palo Alto. No wonder you've had a tough time there." He winked. "You're a California girl. Once I left Iowa for California, I never looked back."

"That's for sure," I said. "Peter wants to be back on the West Coast, too, so that's where he's applying for his residency programs. I'm looking forward to living closer to you guys again."

I had told the Schmidts about my relatively trouble-free pregnancy, but apart from their congratulations we didn't focus on it much. Joanne mostly listened to our dinner conversation with occasional nods. After dinner, she told me about her latest project of making cassette tapes with healing musical tones in collaboration with her identical twin sister (who was a similarly accomplished musician). The idea was to make its therapeutic benefits readily accessible and available to everyone. She gave me a set and suggested I listen to it before my oral defense. The jacket cover was beautiful—a watercolor painting of white water lilies.

"It's designed to calm and realign the nervous system," she said.

Though I was skeptical, I accepted the gift with gratitude.

Throughout the evening, I kept calling her Joanne. As I said goodnight, she said, "I like it better when you call me Mom."

I felt a bit awkward but happy. "Okay, Mom." I gave her a hug and kissed her on the cheek. It was heartwarming to feel so close to her. I headed to the guest bedroom with a big smile on my face.

While lying in bed, it occurred to me that my habit of dissociation had come between Joanne and me. I'd stopped calling her Mom once I moved to Minnesota. After relocating, marrying Peter, and joining his family, I somehow felt I had to emotionally distance myself from the Schmidts. Putting up defensive walls helped suppress my sadness from missing them. It was the only way I knew to protect myself from the pain of separation and alienation from the family who had always been so dear to me. But it was silly. *No need to do that anymore.*

The next day, I headed to Palo Alto to check into the Hotel California. The hotel was quaint, family-owned, and only ten blocks from where I used to live. I booked a two-night stay so that I could have the full day to rest and prepare for my oral defense the following morning and the extra night to wind down before heading back to Minnesota.

After getting settled in my room, I went shopping at my favorite corner grocery. I took a walk along the route I used to take with Shelly, through the narrow path between towering eucalyptus trees, and then up to the hilltop that overlooked the Hewlett Packard campus. I remembered how much Shelly had loved coming here, and I could still visualize her fetching a tennis ball.

The next day, I arrived at the campus an hour before my scheduled defense in Cubberley Hall. I stayed in the car, set aside my skepticism, and listened to one of the music therapy tapes Joanne had given me. It was a series of sustained single tones played on cello or flute, interspersed with prolonged silences. It sounded very simple, but it was serene and meditative. It must have worked because after listening to it for forty minutes, I felt strangely relaxed. It was surreal.

I walked calmly to Cubberley Hall and waited for my thesis committee. One by one they showed up, and although it was part of their job, I felt immensely grateful to this "dream committee" for having served me.

My ethnographic study was largely exploratory and interdisciplinary in nature. I'd conducted classroom observations and interviews with teachers and administrators in Japanese preschools, examining their interpretations and practices of promoting spontaneity and initiative in preschool children. Though relatively foreign to the Japanese at that time, in later years these abstract concepts would become the cornerstone for the promotion of creativity and individuality in Japanese students and the central focus of the educational reform launched by Japan's Ministry of Education in the 1990s.

The panel consisted of five scholars in the fields of educational anthropology, psychology, sociology, and history. One of them, though not officially on my advisory committee, was an internationally renowned pioneer in the field of Japanese studies and had agreed to participate as an adjunct examiner.

I opened my presentation by handing out copies of the *Dilbert* comic strip. Though it oversimplified my findings, it illustrated an important point: Because participants in my study brought their own interpretations and experiences into understanding the abstract concepts of spontaneity and initiative, the Japanese government would face a big challenge in implementing them.

More than halfway through my presentation, my principal thesis advisor handed me a book with an underlined paragraph, asked me to read it, and then comment. I kept my nervousness in check, projected my voice confidently, and read it calmly. I don't recall what it was about, but I remember saying, "It sounds good in theory, but I don't think it quite works like that in practice." I assumed it was the right response since no one objected to it.

After the presentation, I was asked to step out of the room so that the committee could deliberate. I paced the hallway while waiting for their decision. About half an hour later, my advisor came out smiling and said, "Congratulations, you passed. It was unanimous."

I shook his hand and gave him a hug. I felt so grateful, relieved, and liberated that I was tempted to skip through the hallway and out of the building. The last time I'd felt this good about myself was sixteen years earlier at age twenty when I had successfully passed *ikkyu*, the highest-level ski badge test, and received my certification from the Ski Association of Japan.

I drove to Town & Country Village, a strip mall across the street from the campus, to get a celebratory sandwich at my favorite deli. I could hardly contain my elation. Even my harsh, judgmental inner critic stayed quiet and let me savor the victory. I was still in a jovial mood when I stepped inside a little gift shop. I then spotted a familiar face browsing postcards on a rotating display stand. *Wow, former Secretary of State George Shultz! What the heck*, I thought and approached him.

"Hi, Dr. Shultz, nice to meet you," I said and shook his hand. "I just finished my oral defense." I couldn't help but share my happy news with him. I felt as if I knew him from seeing him on TV.

"How did you do?" he asked. "Did you pass?"

"With flying colors."

He smiled. "Congratulations. You must be very proud."

"Thank you. Thank you very much. It was really nice to meet you. Have a great day!" I said and left him to continue browsing postcards.

Everything seemed so perfect. I felt pure joy.

After getting together for supper with a few old friends, I returned to the hotel to share my good news with Peter. I then called Joanne and thanked her for the tape, telling her how it helped me stay calm during the defense. She sounded very happy to hear it.

As I lay in bed that night, I reflected on how I'd managed to pull off the feat. It was a testimony to my commitment, strength, and perseverance, and I was proud of myself. As strange as it may sound, I didn't bother sharing the news with my Japanese family. I didn't think they would have understood the significance of it.

I didn't have an academic job lined up. With the baby coming, there didn't seem to be much point. Besides, I'd learned from both school and my own experience how important the first several years are for a child's development, so I'd already decided to dedicate my efforts to becoming the best mom I could be during that period. Beyond that, I had no idea what I would do. I *hated* competition. The last thing I wanted to worry about was how to get back into academia after a long hiatus.

I felt confident and looked forward to being a mom. There was no way motherhood could be anywhere near as daunting as what I'd just overcome.

Family Secrets

June 2010

In 2010 when my father was ninety, he developed a high fever and became so ill that he almost died. But by the time I rushed from Seattle to Japan to see him in the nursing home, much to our surprise, he'd made a remarkable recovery. He appeared stable, but the attending nurse asked me to keep my visit short because he would get tired. As he had trouble hearing and speaking, I exchanged my greeting with him by writing it down. I then held his hand and he smiled at me, although I wasn't even sure if he knew who I was. He still didn't look well and showed strong signs of dementia. I tried to feed him, but he couldn't swallow, and the food I managed to put into his mouth spilled right out. As I rushed to the nurse's station to get him a wet towel, I burst into tears. He'd changed so dramatically from the tireless surgeon full of vitality I'd grown up with.

"I'll see you tomorrow," I wrote. Then I hugged him and left.

When I went back to Mom's apartment, I felt numb. The reality was sinking in. *He probably won't survive the next health crisis.* A Sado Okesa doll inside the glass cabinet caught my eye. I flashed back to an end-of-year party for Dad's hospital employees I'd attended when I was in elementary school.

During the talent show, he had come onstage wearing a light-blue kimono with an ocean wave design and a funny straw hat that looked like a giant, upside-down taco shell. When the music of Sado Okesa came on, he danced gracefully to the tune. After the dance, he took off the hat and played the harmonica. I remembered how adept he was at *kendo*, the Japanese martial art of fencing, and although I never saw him swim, I heard he was an outstanding swimmer.

Dad always kept his thoughts and feelings largely to himself but was quick to tear up while watching sad TV dramas. He was a humble man but occasionally bragged about having gotten into medical school off the waitlist and then graduating at the top of his class. He was a firm believer in the Japanese cultural value that emphasized effort and diligence over innate abilities. I had always admired him for embodying it.

I went over to the family's Buddhist altar to offer incense to our ancestors. As I sat down, my eyes welled up when I realized I wouldn't chant *Hannya Shingyo* with Dad anymore. *Hannya Shingyo* (the Heart Sutra) captures the essence of the perfect wisdom and the awareness of the true nature of reality and was Dad's favorite. After he'd inherited this fancy Buddhist altar from his father, he chanted this sutra to it every morning and sometimes also in the evening.

Each time I came to visit from the United States, I would sit next to him, hitting the *mokugyo* (a fish-shaped wooden percussion instrument) as he chanted. After the chant, he would crack a huge smile, his small eyes disappearing behind his signature tortoiseshell eyeglasses. I smiled back. It was a seemingly small interaction, but we were happy and content.

One time after we finished chanting, he looked at me pensively and said, with a bit of sadness in his voice, "No matter where you end up living, as long as you're happy, I'll be okay with it." I felt immensely grateful for his support and understanding. I knew how difficult it must have been for him to let his only daughter live so far away.

During this ten-day trip in 2010, my daily visits to Dad were brief, so I still had lots of free time. Even so, I didn't see either of my brothers. Jun-chan was living in Tokyo, leaving his two-story apartment (in the same building Mom lived in) vacant. I had no idea what Hiro-chan was up to. Mom said he hadn't visited her in months, even though he lived in the apartment right below hers. Maybe he was still mad at her. The previous year, when she'd filed for bankruptcy, her financial mishandling had been revealed to the rest of the family, and Hiro-chan had been left to pick up the pieces.

Mom seemed happy to see me, and I was also happy to see her, at least in the beginning. While I managed to stay polite and diplomatic most of the time, every aspect of her behavior provoked a visceral response in me. Whenever she took her dog out for a two-block bathroom walk, she wouldn't dare go without makeup for fear of running into someone she knew. Not that I didn't care about appearance, but her behavior reminded me of the deeper issue that her public image was everything to her and that she prioritized it at the cost of her family life. The same was true of Dad, but I was able to forgive him more easily because of our special bond.

I tried to keep myself busy to avoid interacting with Mom and took advantage of my free time by contacting the Yokohama Harbor Medical Center, where I'd been hospitalized at seventeen. For quite some time, I'd wanted to obtain my patient records and get to the bottom of my so-called illness. Getting information wasn't as easy as I'd expected, however, and required at least ten phone calls and a trip to the hospital with my passport to sign a release form in person.

But I was glad to be able to take care of this bureaucratic procedure. All I had to do now was wait for the records to arrive at my home in Seattle.

One evening, I got together with a friend at an eclectic Taiwanese restaurant. There was a small gift shop inside, and I was drawn to a red-string amulet bracelet. When I found out it symbolized protection, good luck, strength, and connection, I bought it and immediately put it on.

The next day, I reached out to Mr. Tamura, who'd retired from the hospital's business office twenty years earlier. For some uncanny reason he'd always had lots of inside information about our family, and I'd often been curious about it but never asked him why. He was getting old, and as my trips home had become less frequent, I thought this might have been our last chance to talk. During our phone conversation, I was shocked to find out he was actually Mom's cousin.

"My goodness, they haven't told you anything, have they?" he said.

I was even more shocked to learn that my parents had eloped while my dad was still married to someone else. At that time, Mom was eighteen, and Dad was twenty-nine; they'd shunned their relatives ever since. That explained why we seemed to have no extended family.

Mr. Tamura told me Dad's parents had divorced when he was in elementary school. He was separated from his mother and grew up pining for her. His father (Grandpa Masanobu) and stepmother moved from Sado Island to live near us in Sagamihara when Dad was in his mid-forties. I remember occasionally visiting Grandpa's house with my parents. Mom didn't get along with him, and I rarely saw them talk. Dad respected Grandpa and cared about him, but they didn't seem very close. Still, Dad loved to share his fond memories, like going to a mountain with him and catching a varied tit in a wooden cage trap. He also repeatedly said how grateful for and indebted he was to Grandpa's generosity in paying for his medical school.

After getting off the phone with Mr. Tamura, I pieced together the puzzle of my enigmatic Japanese family. My father had a complicated past.

I then remembered a confrontation I'd had with my mother when I was twenty-five and had returned home from California during winter break. Having been in counseling in the United States for a couple of years, I had gained more insight into my family and myself, but my festering resentment toward my mother had impeded my healing.

It started with our typical standoff, the two of us glaring at each other across the kitchen table. This was in our old house where the kitchen was not especially inviting but more like a place to fulfill the biological need of hunger. A built-in cabinet housed a small TV, and at that time, like always, it was on.

"You are so spoiled and ungrateful," Mom said. "Don't you see how fortunate you are to have grown up in this family, always getting anything you wanted?" She was dressed casually in a skirt and cashmere sweater, but her face was immaculately made up.

"Of course I do," I said, "I'm very grateful for that. But I also needed more family connection, emotional connection. That's why I ended up in the hospital. Didn't my doctors tell you that?"

She snorted. "When you were in the hospital, the doctors said you were overcoddled and spoiled. That's why you're prone to stress and shock. You can't deal with adversity."

"That's not what they told me. They blamed it on my home environment." I threw up my hands. "It's not even worth discussing this anymore." But then I had a light-bulb moment. "What about your childhood? Were you as lonely as I was? Did you ever feel abandoned and totally alone?"

She was quiet for a while as she stared at the opened bags of snacks on the table—rice crackers, cookies, chocolates—many of which were stale. Then she started to sob. "I'm sorry I wasn't there for you . . . I was young and lonely too. Your dad worked so hard that I hardly ever saw him."

My mother knew how to work tears to her advantage, but this time it seemed different. Genuine. When I asked her to tell me about her childhood, she said her mother had died from childbirth-related complications when she was only a year old. She and her older sister were sent away to live with relatives until she was ten, and her father got remarried. When she was sixteen, her sister contracted tuberculosis and died while being hospitalized for pleurisy. She lost her father when she was thirty-three.

I was silent for a while, processing all this new information. She'd been surrounded by death. It explained her over-the-top reaction to death rituals.

I asked her whether she felt sad, lonely, or angry, but she said everyone had treated her nicely, so she had no bad memories. When I pressed her for more details, she became angry and said, "Why do you want to know such things? It creeps me out. I don't remember anymore."

Maybe she didn't want to revisit her past because it was too painful, or maybe she really didn't remember—I didn't know. What was clear was that she'd been quite alone, and I remember her sometimes saying, "*Tengai kodoku*," when she was feeling sad and seemed lost in thought. *I'm all alone in the world.*

Back when I was around twenty-five, my anger toward her seemed to have loosened its grip, and the toxic feelings inside me were washed away. But now, decades later, I found it an ongoing challenge to be kind and compassionate toward her, especially whenever she got on my nerves.

Both my parents' unusual upbringings had likely arrested their development and caused them to behave like children with unmet emotional needs. How could they have given us proper parental guidance when they'd never received it themselves? How would they have known how to be a family when they didn't have the slightest clue what it would take to build one? If I hadn't met the Schmidts, I would never have known how close a family could and should be or what kind of family I wanted to make.

Before flying back to Seattle, I went to see Dad one last time to say goodbye. I still couldn't tell whether he recognized me. I was hesitant to part with the red-string amulet bracelet I'd just bought, but I took it off and put it on his wrist, telling him about its symbolism of strength and connection. I wanted to give him something tangible to remember me by. He looked puzzled at first but then smiled, so I assumed he was happy to receive it.

Demystifying My "Illness"

August 2010

For decades I had buried the nightmarish experience of being hauled to a psychiatric hospital at age seventeen—that period of utter chaos and confusion, inward and outward. How on earth had I gotten myself into that quagmire? I wanted to get to the bottom of it.

Two months after the trip to see my ailing father in Japan, a box of documents from the university hospital arrived at my Seattle home. I was initially overwhelmed by the hundreds of pages of doctors' and nurses' notes, but I tackled page after page over a period of a few weeks.

I was shocked to discover the doctors had suspected schizophrenia, citing symptoms such as manic behavior, delusion, hallucinations, aggression, insomnia, and a refusal to eat. During the course of treatment, the diagnosis evolved from schizophrenia to suspicion of schizophrenia to schizoaffective disorder, and then "schizo-ish," to mood disorder, depression, and *shinshinsho* (stress-induced psychosomatic disorder). They couldn't seem to determine which illness I had. Regardless, I'd been treated—under the assumption of schizophrenia—with heavy-duty antipsychotics.

Evidently, there had been tremendous confusion, misunderstanding, miscommunication, and overinterpretation between the medical staff and me from the beginning. I'd woken up in a strange hospital room with zero understanding of why I was there and what was going on. And because I was still feeling residual anger and aggression toward anyone I perceived as a threat, I was hostile toward doctors and nurses who tried to make me do things against my will, like swallowing a bunch of pills three times a day or receiving shots.

For their part, the doctors and nurses monitored, evaluated, and scrutinized my behavioral minutiae, sometimes to the point of overinterpretation. As they paid particular attention to my moodiness, irritability, restlessness, talkativeness, and hyperactivity, they often categorized and evaluated my behaviors as symptoms of my "illness" (whatever it was that week) with regression (–) or progress (+) markers. Being defiant, noncompliant, and refusing medications were definitely no-nos.

If not seen through a pathologizing lens, my behaviors, such as aggression, hostility, irritability, and yelling, would all (with the exception of the attempted kick) fit the description of an emotionally troubled, rebellious teenager.

Other notes read more like an evaluation of manners: eating too much of one thing or another; eating too little; eating with mouth open; eating while walking or talking; overindulging in junk food; talking or laughing loudly; interrupting someone; keeping a disorganized room; sleeping in an unladylike manner; wearing a poor choice of clothes; and being too curt, rude, inconsiderate, irritable, or moody. What if all these "transgressions" had been the result of being too drugged and feeling sluggish? What if I'd been sick of answering how many times I'd been to the bathroom each day?

Among the nurses who were sticklers for etiquette, one had

repeatedly caught me wandering the hallways, stuffing handfuls of chips into my mouth. "You're seventeen," she'd call out, her tone contemptuous. "Act your age!"

I frequently came across the description "immature for her age" because they'd categorized my high-pitched voice as a childish way of ingratiating myself with others to obtain favors. The mannerisms that my classmates had called cute were my baseline idiosyncrasies, but the nurses deemed them annoying and unacceptable. I don't think I was behaving that way on purpose, but it might also be true that I had unconsciously regressed into childish ways of speaking and acting while in the hospital.

Perusing my medical records, I was horrified by the doctors' trial-and-error approach to the antipsychotics they'd given me—frequently switching medications, adjusting dosages, adding this, taking away that, all of which required my brain to constantly readjust to the chemicals and their effects. They'd treated me like a lab rat. No wonder I'd felt so discombobulated. I mentioned this to Peter, and he suspected it might have permanently messed up my GI tract too. Knowing my sensitivity to drugs in general, it was unsurprising that during treatment and recovery, not only did I not respond, but my condition worsened, with a host of debilitating side effects, such as dizziness, declining eyesight, and perennial brain fog.

However, flipping through the hundreds of pages of my patient records, I was equally surprised to find the revelatory comments written by some doctors based on a series of interviews they'd conducted with my visitors. Through them, our family dysfunction came to light, and they developed insights into what might have gone wrong with me.

Dr. Asano wrote, "The more I find out about her family environment, the more bizarre it is. Her family members are totally *barabara*. Might be no surprise that she developed her current symptoms."

Dr. Kato wrote, "The cause of the Pat's [patient's] problems is rooted in her family. When I interviewed one of her brothers, he said the family never eats together, even on weekends, and gets together maybe once or twice a year, but that doesn't bother him . . . Her mother especially is a real piece of work. She seems totally out of touch with her daughter even though she calls the hospital many times a day to inquire about the Pat's status, regardless of the hour or how annoying it is . . . When interviewing the parents, their facial expressions suddenly became lively as they spoke about their upcoming foreign travel for Rotary Club governors, and their minds seemed totally preoccupied with it. I got the impression that was more important for them than discussing their daughter's prognosis. When I brought up the Pat's issue of loneliness, the mother quickly shifted to talking about herself, saying angrily, 'I'm lonely too!'"

His observation explains a few intriguing comments he'd made during the course of my treatment: "Your family isn't normal," or "You have no real home to return to, isn't that right?"

Dr. Oki wrote, "Upon returning from America, the Pat continued making efforts to become independent. The more keenly aware she became of the abnormality and absurdity of her family or of the feeling that she wasn't loved by her mother as a child, the more psychologically isolated she became. Then she started developing delusional thinking that if she attended a church, God would rescue and protect her or that her American host family would come to see her at church."

Dr. Oki concluded, "Triggered by some kind of culture shock, the Pat became strongly motivated to change her former dependency [on her parents] and to become more independent, which in turn created her psychological isolation from her family. She then became very confused and didn't know what to do anymore. When I pay more attention to what she's saying now, she has a clear insight into the process that led her to where she is. At any rate, I came to conclude that whatever she might be ailing from, her illness is pretty mild."

I was surprised to read such incisive comments written by him only eighteen days after my hospital admission. His attentiveness and careful observation contrasted sharply with the approach of many of the other doctors, who tended to pathologize me and stick with their judgments seemingly based on their first impression, compartmentalizing my behavior into preexisting boxes.

It was clear I'd been the victim of misdiagnosis and mismanagement, both of which led to the heavy-handed psychiatric treatment I received. Typical of psychiatry in Japan in the late 1970s, my doctors administered a primitive, one-size-fits-all treatment by first knocking me out with powerful antipsychotics and then painstakingly tapering off those meds. And, I understood now, that wasn't my fault.

I've asked three psychiatrists in Seattle if I might have schizophrenia, and they all reassured me I don't. They concluded I had likely developed a brief psychotic disorder (or reactive psychosis) and temporarily developed symptoms such as hallucinations and delusion—hallmarks of schizophrenia—following the week of sleep deprivation.

Perhaps all I'd needed was some medication to help me sleep and an insightful, compassionate human being who could listen to me and understand what I'd been going through.

Morning Heaven

April 2014

It was close to midnight. David was doing his homework in his room. After being in family therapy for nearly five months, we'd sharpened our parenting skills, and the yelling in the house had dissipated. Since we'd agreed not to fuss over David's bedtime anymore, I went down simply to say goodnight. The treadmill no longer doubled as a hamper. The television was off. And yet, when he looked up from his desk, there were tears in his eyes.

"What's wrong?"

"I'm really overwhelmed, Mom. I still have so much homework, and I also have to study for my math test," he said. "I'm so stressed, my skin is breaking out. Will you call the dermatologist's office and make an appointment for me? Also, I'm sick of having to avoid tree nuts all the time, and I'd like to know if I might have outgrown that food allergy."

"Okay," I said, "I'll take care of that for you tomorrow."

"Also, I'm getting tired of the same old breakfast. I need fewer carbs and more protein."

"Okay. I'll fix you something different tomorrow morning."

Bombarded with these random requests, I was a bit taken aback. But then I realized this was a sure sign of stress—it amplified his tendency to focus on the negative.

When he realized I wasn't lashing out and nagging him to go to bed and was willing to accommodate his requests, his shoulders softened. "Thanks, Mom."

I hesitated. "You've been doing great this year and have already earned enough extra credit for your hard work, so even if you let things slide this time, it shouldn't affect your overall grades. Don't worry about it, okay? I wish I could stay up and keep you company, but I need to go to sleep." I gave him a hug and said goodnight.

The next morning, I jumped out of bed to avoid being blasted by David's alarm and went into the kitchen to prepare something new for him. *Hmm, what kind of breakfast would be protein-rich?* In the refrigerator, I spotted a package of teriyaki-flavored tofu. I minced garlic and ginger and chopped up onions, snap peas, peppers, asparagus, celery, and carrots, along with the tofu.

As I sautéed the garlic and ginger, the aroma wafted through the kitchen. I threw in the remaining ingredients with a teaspoon of umami powder to enhance the flavor. Then, as a finishing touch, I added a dash of Trader Joe's Island Soyaki Sauce, and voilà! I'd created a hearty breakfast with good protein. I wasn't sure what David would think of it; he'd never eaten such an elaborate breakfast before.

Food had never been important in my Japanese family. Its main purpose was to fulfill the biological need of hunger. Sit-down breakfasts were especially rare. I remember being in fourth or fifth grade and sitting at the kitchen table while my mother frantically yanked and braided my waist-length hair. I accidentally spilled my miso soup, and much of it landed on my navy-blue winter school uniform skirt. She was furious. With no spare uniform on hand, she sent me to school with my soup-soaked clothing. The clammy wetness grossed me out so much I could hardly concentrate on my schoolwork. And the smell not only nauseated me but also made me feel self-conscious and humiliated.

My bento box lunch had never been anything to look forward to either. While other kids' mothers competed over who could make the most elaborate and nutritious lunch, my two-sectioned Tupperware container's ratio of rice to *okazu* (side dishes) was eighty/twenty. The rice had a small, pickled red plum in the center to make *hinomaru*, the Japanese flag. The *okazu* usually consisted of a single vegetable like boiled spinach or pickled daikon radish and whatever was left over from the night before, such as chicken katsu, croquette, or squid cut into strips. Yes, squid!

A classmate once pointed to my lunch and said, "Eww! Shige-chan's eating *slug* again!"

As I became increasingly self-conscious about opening my bento box in public, I complained to my mom, and then she refused to make me lunch altogether.

She delegated lunch duty to "Grandma" Aiko. Grandma Aiko wasn't related to us but had married my Grandpa Masanobu to be a live-in housekeeper and caregiver after his second wife had died. Grandma Aiko was at least ten years younger than Grandpa. She was an impressive woman full of vitality and a culinary expert who used to teach cooking classes. Her lunches were nothing short of amazing. The ratio of rice to *okazu* was reversed to twenty/eighty. The lunch resembled a festive mini *osechi*, the Japanese celebratory New Year's cuisine, with a dozen colorful and nutritious varieties of *okazu*—vegetables, fish, meat, and other proteins. Everybody marveled at the radical transformation of my bento lunch.

For a while I enjoyed this over-the-top lunch. But Grandma Aiko had to get up at five every morning to make it and then walk over to Sagamihara Station to hand it to me. Although she didn't live far from the station and seemed happy doing this for me, at some point I thought it was asking too much of her. One day I politely declined the offer, saying I'd buy lunch on the way to school, but I never forgot her kindness and generous labor of love.

At 7:30 a.m., I went to David's room to get him out of bed. As usual, his alarm clock was blasting. I turned it down and nudged his shoulder to get him up. "David, I made a great breakfast for you this morning. Come look."

No reaction.

"You said you wanted a protein-rich breakfast. It'll get cold if you don't hurry."

He didn't like when food meant to be served warm got cold, so he slowly rolled out of bed. As he entered the kitchen, he rubbed his eyes and saw the wholesome breakfast sitting on the island.

His eyes opened wide. "That looks really good, Mom. Thanks."

"You're welcome. Go take a shower, and I'll have your breakfast on the tray so you can eat it in the car."

I peeked into the bathroom while he brushed his teeth and said, "I'll wait for you in the car." We were able to leave a few minutes before 8:00 a.m., a remarkable feat.

As we drove to school, David ate the breakfast, looking happy, and we listened to a Mozart concerto on the radio. He finished the entire bowl before we arrived and thanked me again before getting out of the car.

Wow, that worked well. No yelling, no arguing, no clenched teeth. What a pleasant morning this was.

While I waited for the light to change, gentle rays of sunshine poked through the clouds. A huge Bud Light semitruck beside me sported a giant Seahawks logo along with the phrase, "It is the sure sign of a good time." I was feeling so optimistic that I took this as a divine message from heaven.

Thereafter, things at home stayed relatively calm and peaceful. A few days before Mother's Day, I was in for a real surprise. David came into the kitchen to tell me he'd just watched a forty-five-minute home video from when he was a toddler. He realized how much he'd been loved and cared for and teared up as he apologized for his angry comments and behavior over the past nine months. My jaw dropped. *Really? Was that all it took for him to reach this conclusion?* Just as he had turned into an adolescent hormonal monster overnight on his sixteenth birthday, he snapped back into a reflective, thoughtful teenager.

That Mother's Day was beyond anything I could have imagined. In the morning, before I came down to the kitchen, David and Liz fixed a pancake breakfast with fruit and yogurt on the side and a cup of coffee, which they set on the table next to an arrangement of carnations and a card. In the card was a sweet, thoughtful message about how much he loved me and appreciated my strength and tenacity to forge ahead no matter what was happening in my life. Liz also wrote me a nice note expressing similar sentiments.

As my heart opened, my grip on the resentment and frustration I'd been holding against Liz loosened. When I mentioned my concern about her seeing her mother, she reassured me they'd had an early Mother's Day celebration.

"Thank you," I said, and gave them each a big tight hug.

As we ate, I asked David if he thought, as I did, that the family therapy had been worth it.

"Not really," he said. "I don't think it helped me that much, but you talking about yourself did. You had a really difficult childhood. I had no idea."

My oversharing hadn't backfired this time—it had helped.

David went on to say he admired how hard I'd strived to overcome many of my childhood adversities. "You have a lot of inner strength."

There had been many past Mother's Days that I felt I hadn't deserved. I was often very critical of myself and felt like a failure as a mother. But this time I thought it was a well-merited celebration, especially after all the hard work I'd put in to repair our relationship and regain David's trust. I was happy to reach this positive turning point with him.

The trick would be to make it last.

The Closing Family Counseling Session

May 15, 2014

Because things continued to improve at home, we switched to a maintenance schedule with counseling. I became more optimistic and confident in the parenting department by keeping calm and trusting David more. Counseling had also helped me realize that my overreactions to and overprotectiveness of David were not just about wanting to spare him from hardship—I had also wanted to avoid being triggered by the memories of my hospitalization. But in doing so, I might have jeopardized his own development.

Enrolling in a twelve-week writing class helped to ground me and shift my focus, and I became less consumed by the ongoing saga at home. By early May we decided to bring counseling to a close.

At the final session, I showed up solo to Janice's office with a notepad and pen, ready to jot down any remaining advice she had to offer. The spring sunlight coming through the window lit up the tree of life. I thanked her fervently for her helpfulness, saying how impressed I'd been by her expertise. Then, half-afraid and half-curious, I asked her what she thought of our family.

She tapped her pencil as she gathered her thoughts. "Nice family." She paused. "Yeah, nice family."

"Really? How?"

"Because you love each other very much," she said, "and care about each other very deeply."

"That's nice of you to say. Thank you." Why couldn't I see that? I found her insight reassuring. She wasn't the kind of person who would say things just to make me feel good.

She knew I'd essentially grown up motherless and that in my attempts to be the best mother I could be, I'd ended up overcompensating. Any unexpected complications or setbacks had easily overwhelmed and frightened me.

"It was a perfect storm," I said. "All too easy to neglect myself."

"Do you know how to take care of yourself now?" she asked.

In the awkward silence that followed, I looked at her blankly and realized I had no idea how to move forward. Desperate for something to say, I told her about the recent tofu breakfast and the day I'd dubbed "morning heaven."

"I learned that if I operate from a place of love and compassion instead of ego, things can't go too wrong."

She set down her notepad. "You just said something brilliant."

I was buoyed by such rare praise from her. "Really? Let me write it down before I forget it."

Within seconds, her face grew stern, but I didn't know what might have triggered the sudden shift. "Why don't you step up and be the adult? Your family would be much happier. You seem so comfortable hiding in the corner and just observing. What are you waiting for?

Do you think if you stay in that powerless place, your mom will show up?"

I was so surprised by the brusque comment that I clenched my pen tightly and said nothing. *What does she mean? Is she saying that my family is unhappy because of me? Is it all my fault? Do I really hold the key to change all this?* But I was too intimidated to ask her to explain herself.

Later, after giving it more thought, I assumed she'd been chastising me for lacking personal agency and for my not-so-secret desire to depend on some authority or maternal figure in general, not my mother per se. Maybe this had been building up inside her for some time and she'd wanted to point it out to me once and for all—my reluctance to recognize my power in the family—and here I'd turned over my power again, asking her to judge my family.

I was sad that we ended on a sour note. It defeated my original intention of wrapping up the final session with a positive sense of closure. I couldn't bear for another maternal figure to be critical of me, but it was too late.

Upon leaving, I asked if it would be okay to contact her should I need her assistance again. It seemed like the diplomatic thing to say. She said yes. I felt awful for having offended her, no matter how unintentional it was, and left the office disappointed. But my unsettled feelings came from more than this awkward parting. On one hand, I was relieved not to have to come back again, for I'd grown tired of dealing with her blunt and sometimes abrasive style. On the other hand, I wasn't sure I was ready to navigate these uncharted waters alone.

Wallaby to the Rescue

October 2014

About five months after ending family counseling, I was under the illusion that we were over the hump and that our family peace had been restored, though Peter and I hadn't yet formed a united front in our parenting and were making even slower progress in the marriage department. But we'd managed to put into practice the tips we'd learned, communicating and negotiating more constructively, and I'd learned to keep my temper in check and to pause before speaking so that I could cool down.

Operating from a place of love and compassion? Not so much.

A different kind of stress was mounting—this time from David's college applications. He had entered the make-or-break junior year and had recently been officially diagnosed with ADHD. I wasn't sure how toxic this combination might become, and my fear was exacerbated by the suspicion that David was planning his entire future around his ongoing romance with Liz. I knew in my gut this would be a mistake.

As my worries over his welfare intensified, so did the tension in our family. During particularly stressful times, I felt tempted by my childhood coping strategy: getting a soft, cuddly pet. My body couldn't tolerate alcohol, and I didn't want to smoke pot (which was legal in Washington State), so getting a cute animal seemed like a wholesome alternative.

Even though David and Liz had been together for a year, I still wasn't comfortable with the weekend sleepovers at our house. Liz was a sweet girl, but her emotional fragility and never-ending crises had convinced me she was too much of a burden for David.

By stark contrast, Liz's mother, Diane, who'd married her high school sweetheart, was convinced her daughter and my son were meant for each other. She did everything in her power to keep the relationship going by pushing for more frequent weekend adoptions at her house. Peter and I spent many weekends alone in Seattle while our son was ninety miles away with his newly adopted family. At times we felt like our nest was already empty. I must have let my guard down to allow this to happen against the therapist's advice, but it was exhausting to keep pushing back against all the forces against us.

I found it appalling but not surprising when Diane hinted one day that David and her daughter should attend the same college. She even offered to chaperone out-of-state college campus visits. It was time to put my foot down. But how? I didn't know.

That night as we were getting ready for bed, I said to Peter, "They're way too young to have their futures planned out like that."

Though he agreed Diane's suggestion of joint college tours was inappropriate, he said, "You're worrying way too much. There's no way they'll end up at the same college or get married. David is a good kid and a good student. He's very ambitious and works hard, and he doesn't drink, use drugs, or hang out with the wrong crowd—not like my sister. Cut him some slack."

Peter often measured David against his sister, who had run away from home at age sixteen and moved in with her twenty-year-old boyfriend one thousand miles away in Long Island. She developed an addiction to quaaludes and ended up in inpatient rehab at seventeen. At twenty she went to prison for selling drugs. He was nine when all this began, and he witnessed firsthand his family being torn apart.

"She put my parents through hell," he said, "and there was a tremendous amount of yelling in the house. He's a good kid, so quit worrying about him."

Yes, David's issues were nothing compared to what he'd been through, but I didn't see it that way. David's choice of college was critical. Comparing him to such an extreme case was both irrelevant and unhelpful.

Thinking of this now, I can understand Peter's reaction. I, too, had lived through a painful family situation, even worse than his, so I couldn't help seeing situations through my own distorted lens. We were both quite stubborn, each insisting on being right and intolerant of the other's views. It had only been five months since our last counseling session, but we'd already forgotten the therapist's advice to stay united.

I went on the offensive, criticizing Peter's laissez-faire style of parenting. "Remember what Janice told us? We *tell* him if he isn't acting in his best interest. Obviously, he doesn't know how to make good decisions for himself. If we don't step in, he might make really bad decisions that will affect his future."

But Peter didn't budge. To be the only one freaking out and seeing what I perceived as obvious warning signs made me feel dismissed, lonely, and kind of sick—the old familiar pain from my childhood of being ignored. My long-smoldering frustration and resentment had created such prickly feelings toward Peter that I snapped. "You treat him like your buddy, as if he's an adult. But he still needs us to set limits and boundaries. Why don't you do something? Don't be a chump."

"Don't call me that." He stood next to his dresser and crossed his arms. "I'm not a chump."

"Then step up and join me. I can't fight this alone. You come from a more normal family than I do. You should know better. Don't make me the bad cop all the time." My jaw clenched and my lips quivered as I fought back angry tears.

The next morning, I still hadn't fully recovered from the previous night's argument. Worrying about David's lack of sleep, mood swings, and tendency to overcommit and burn himself out only elevated my stress level. Yet, I felt powerless to change any of it. In that moment, I regressed to a childlike state of mind and finally succumbed to my urgent need for the potent antidote. *What the heck, might as well.*

As soon as Peter walked into the kitchen, I blurted out, "I want to get a wallaby from the kangaroo farm."

His eyes opened wide. "Okay, let's go get one."

I was delighted by how game he was to go along with my whim. Maybe he wanted me to be happy for a change. It was a crisp autumn morning, the sky clear, the leaves bright red, yellow, and orange. We hopped into his car and set off for the kangaroo farm.

My love affair with wallabies began in the summer of 1978 when I turned seventeen and met a pet wallaby that belonged to a family in the outback town of Echuca, Australia. I still have a photo of him taking a slice of apple from my hand. I was grinning as if I couldn't contain my giddiness. Since then, I'd fantasized about a pint-size kangaroo hopping around my house. And then recently, watching a local TV show, Peter and I learned that baby wallabies were available for adoption only an hour's drive north of our home.

"I want one," I said to Peter at the time.

"That would be kinda cool," he said.

I found his response surprising and heartening. Usually, he was Mr. Frugal (from the humble Midwest) and Mr. Sensible (except maybe when parenting our teenager). If he didn't think owning an exotic pet was a far-fetched fantasy, well, maybe it wasn't.

Within an hour I was cradling a joey in my arms. My heart quivered with joy. At seven months old and weighing only four pounds, he looked like a cross between a giant mouse and a fawn. He had innocent, dark-brown doe eyes, long eyelashes, velvety ears, soft, grayish-brown fur, and a long, fleecy tail. His silky fur smelled like hay, a comforting, earthy smell that made me feel reassured and grounded in the present moment.

I handed a check for $1,200.00 to the owner of the farm, who was also coincidentally named Joey. While she gathered fleece pouches, feeding bottles, formula, kangaroo pellets, and hay, we had a small chat.

"What are you going to name him?" she asked.

"Hmm . . . Wally the wallaby?" I looked over at Peter.

He nodded.

I then mentioned our dogs. "Would they and Wally be okay together?"

"You'll have to keep an eye on your dogs . . . but if things don't work out, it's okay to bring him back," she said somewhat reluctantly.

I was unsure of how Biscuit, our seventy-pound Goldendoodle, would react to the newcomer. Still, it was one of those moments when the overpowering feelings clouded rational judgment, and I dismissed the potential challenges. Welcoming this adorable critter into the home could provide the ultimate pet therapy to de-stress and might even help bring my family together.

When we returned with Wally nestled in my arms, David's jaw dropped. He grew excited to the point of hyperventilating and became the sweet little boy I used to know.

"Thank you, Mom. Thank you. He's so cute. I'll be the coolest kid in the whole school."

It made me happy to see him so animated and full of joy.

Living with Wally was like having a newborn again. The first couple of days were relatively uneventful. I kept him contained in a playpen much of the time, except when I bottle-fed him or carried him in a baby sling. He wasn't all that interested in eating the kangaroo pellets but seemed to enjoy almonds and pecans, as well as freeze-dried kale, dried apricots, pumpkin dog biscuits, and Honeycrisp apples. Our new baby had expensive tastes. My heart melted each time he licked my hands with his itty-bitty tongue as if to say, "I love you to death." Holding him or just watching him sleep so peacefully in my arms helped me forget the family strife and feel more at ease and comforted than I'd felt in years.

I reminisced a lot about the days when David had been sweet and innocent like Wally. I flashed back to his adorable grin when I used to nurse him. He'd stare up at me, open his mouth, and smile playfully. It made me laugh and created a warm bond with him. I wondered if my mother had ever felt that way with me.

One evening when David and Peter came home, we all spent time together playing with Wally. We let him hop around downstairs in our family room.

"Go, Wally, go!" we shouted as he darted around furniture as if on an obstacle course. One of us had to calm Biscuit, who reacted to Wally's swift, nimble movements by barking and trying to push through the makeshift barricade.

Together we laughed at Wally's humorous antics. When frightened, he'd stick his head inside the fleece pouch that we'd hung in his pen and freeze like a statue. Although his body was fully exposed, he must have thought, *If I can't see you, you can't see me.* It had been so long since we'd shared so much fun. My heart softened at the flickering moments of hope that we could once again be a happy, united family.

Once Wally had tasted freedom, though, he didn't want to settle back into the playpen. Even past midnight, he refused to go back inside the fleece pouch. "C'mon, Wally," I coaxed, "hop in. Get back into the pouch, *pleeease.*" It took him a good forty-five minutes to finally calm down and settle back inside.

On the evening of day three, Peter came home from work, looked at me, and chuckled. "You look like crap."

I looked in the bathroom mirror and was aghast at my appearance—uncombed hair, no makeup, and bags under my eyes from not having slept much for the past few nights. I'd worn the same striped T-shirt for three days in a row and was still in my pajama pants. It was a lot like my early motherhood days. *I'm way too old to be doing this.* I no longer had the stamina to handle a high-maintenance child.

By day four, I felt increasingly tired and restless from sleep deprivation and being cooped up in the house all day trying to keep Wally safe. So, I emailed a dozen friends, adding, "Meet our newest family member, Wally!" to the subject line and attached a photo of Wally and my disheveled self.

"For real? Is that a kangaroo?" a friend in California asked.

"Wally is so cute! Where did you get him?" an animal lover friend in Minnesota wanted to know. "How big will he get? What's his life expectancy? Does he need to be potty-trained? What do your dogs think of him?"

"I see now where your son's passionate nature comes from," a friend in Seattle wrote. "It's from you."

But what stood out most was a response from a friend in Colorado. "The little guy is so cute, but he belongs in a large preserve with other wallabies. He's going to add more stress to your already stressful situation at home. You've been worrying about your son's tendency to overextend himself, but guess who he learned that from?"

What if she's right? Questions raced through my mind. *What if our dogs get sick? What if Wally gets sick? What about our house and backyard hummingbirds?* I hadn't changed the nectar for over a week. And then there was my marriage. That needed more attention too.

On day five, more exhaustion set in. I'd been up much of the night calming down Wally, who kept banging against the pen while trying to jump out. I began to feel buyer's remorse, wondering what the future might hold for us. I spent time online trying to find a wallaby support group, but to no avail. Instead, I came across an old article in the *Seattle Times* about a fifteen-year-old boy in Woodinville, Washington, who'd raised a baby wallaby named Marley. After some detective work, I found the phone number of the boy's mother, Colleen.

Colleen said the family had adopted Marley when he was a baby. But after living in the house for two years, Marley was killed by the family dog. As she told me the story, I became increasingly worried about Wally's safety. Biscuit still hadn't warmed up to him and seemed ready to pounce at any moment.

"Marley was dumb as a post," she said. "We had to put him in adult diapers that needed to be changed three or four times a day. He also jumped up everywhere. One night, he got up on the kitchen counter and gobbled up an entire plate of cookies, knocking down everything else with his huge tail. It was mayhem."

Oh no! Wally jumping up on things had been one of my fears. I imagined spending all day cleaning up after he'd wreaked havoc in our house.

"Marley was cute and sweet when he was a baby," Colleen said, "and he bonded with my son, but once he grew to be about fifty pounds, everything about him became a tremendous amount of work." She paused. "I wouldn't recommend it to anyone."

That was the final blow. I was convinced Wally had to go back to the farm or I would make my life a whole lot more complicated than it already was. Thank goodness he'd come with a money-back guarantee. Both David and Peter were disappointed at first, but they understood it was the right decision.

I was a little afraid of upsetting the owner of the kangaroo farm, Joey, when I called to tell her we wanted to return Wally. She sounded disappointed but said that she understood. That night when David told his friends we were returning Wally the next day, four of them showed up to say goodbye to him. They all commented on how incredibly precious Wally was. They let him hop around in David's room and then took turns carrying Wally in the front-loading baby carrier, snapping photos with him.

While eating a slice of pizza, David's friend Ben said, "I'm already attached to him. I'll be sad to see him go."

What a sweet thing to say. I hadn't realized that seventeen-year-old boys, who usually put on such a facade of toughness, could exhibit such tenderness toward a baby animal. Above all, I was delighted to see David reconnect with his friends. I'd missed seeing them at our house during the past year, as David had prioritized his time with Liz and seemingly ditched them.

On day seven, a Saturday, Peter had to attend a medical conference, so I asked David to drive me to the farm. I sat in the passenger seat, cradling Wally on my lap. From time to time, David reached over to stroke Wally's head, and Wally responded by licking his hand.

"He's so cute," he said. "Do we really have to return him?"

"Yes," I said. "He'll be much happier roaming free with other wallabies." I felt a strange sense of relief at having caught my misjudgment before it was too late. But more than that, I felt like an adult. I remembered Janice's admonishment to step up and be the adult. This must have been what she'd meant: recognizing that I'd made a mistake, owning it, and then making the hard decisions to correct it.

Once we got to the farm, the human Joey greeted us in a less joyous manner than she had on my previous visit. She looked haggard, the front of her shirt stained. I felt a little nervous as she invited us into her dimly lit house. It was in total disarray and reeked of animal urine. There were many small kangaroo figurines and knickknacks, as well as several portraits of kangaroos displayed on the walls and tables. With a sad face, David handed over Wally, still nesting inside the brown fleece pouch.

We were startled by a shriek coming from upstairs. Then a stocky bird hopped down the steps.

"Oh my God," I said. "Is that a kookaburra?" I remembered that loud signature laughing sound. "I saw a kookaburra in Australia when I was seventeen." I felt like a child again. *Hmm, a free-roaming kookaburra.* I then wondered what it might be like to have one hopping around our house.

But that fantasy was immediately dashed when Joey brought it over to show us, and it crapped on the floor. "Oh, you naughty bird," she said, and put it back on the staircase.

I thanked her for letting us try Wally at home for a week. "We totally adore him, but we became very worried about his safety because of our dog. I truly appreciate your kindness and understanding."

She handed me my check. I gave back Wally's belongings, along with $120.00 in cash, joking that it was a 10 percent restocking fee and a donation to her farm.

The trip home presented a rare opportunity to discuss things with David.

"Thanks for doing all the driving today," I said. "Are you sad about Wally?"

"Yes," he said.

"Me too. But I'm also feeling quite relieved to have returned him, or we might have been in a pickle."

The classical music on the radio settled me, as did the rural landscape we drove through, though I felt sheepish for having exposed my childish coping mechanism. After an awkward moment of silence between us, I said, "How could I possibly have thought nothing could go wrong with having a wallaby in our house? So impulsive and stupid. As your mom, I'm supposed to model sensible behavior for you. I'm not a very good mom. I'm sorry."

David said, "No, you're a good mom."

I wasn't convinced. "You think I'm making progress in becoming a better mom?"

He nodded.

I smiled and squeezed his hand. "Does Liz complain about her mom as much as you complain about me? Diane seems like a perfect mother."

"Yeah, a lot," he said.

A strange sense of relief swept over me. Maybe I'd been wrong to assume Diane had breezed through her daughter's treacherous adolescence. Maybe we were all in the same boat, scrambling to understand and deal with our teenagers. The resentment I'd been feeling toward her softened just a little.

My Father's Funeral

January 2015

Two months had passed since I'd sent Wally back to the farm. On the family front things had improved, though I still had good days and bad days, depending on my quality of sleep and my neck and lower back pain. In managing my chronic pain, I'd opted for alternative medicine like chiropractic care, acupuncture, and massage instead of resorting to cortisone shots or surgery. Despite my efforts, though, the pain flared up, especially when I was under stress.

"Your mom left you a voicemail," Peter said, when I returned from my weekly acupuncture appointment.

I immediately listened to her message. In a shaky, barely audible voice, she said in Japanese, "Dad has just passed away. Please call me."

I was speechless for a moment, then numb, but strangely, not a single tear fell from my eyes. I'd known his death was coming—he'd been in the nursing home for several years. Peter walked into the kitchen and saw me standing with my shoulders slumped, face blank.

"Dad passed away," I said, stunned.

He came over to hug me. "I'm so sorry."

I hugged him back. My dad had died one month shy of his

ninety-fourth birthday. "He lived a long time, but his quality of life just wasn't there, so . . . it was time for him to go."

My dad's death was something I had dreaded. I had nightmares about him dying, though I'd never been as concerned about my mom dying. Now that it had happened, it seemed surreal. It was no longer a nightmare or an eventuality, but real and absolutely final.

I knew Peter was genuinely sympathetic and sad for me, as he, too, had recently lost his father. When he'd flown back to Minnesota to see him before he died, he had told me how shocked and heartbroken he'd been to see his father so emaciated, his body ravaged by melanoma. He'd called me from the hospice partway through his visit and broke down and cried over the phone. It was only the third time I'd heard him cry in our twenty-two years of marriage. The first was when we'd lost Shelly, and the second was when our beloved golden retriever Nikki passed.

It was 5:00 p.m., and with the seventeen-hour time difference, it would be 10:00 a.m. on Sunday in Japan. I gathered my strength to call home. My brother answered the phone.

"Jun-chan?" It was funny that I still called him Jun-chan even though he was fifty-eight years old. "Chan" is a suffix commonly attached to children's names or used among family members.

"Oh, Chako." He sounded disheartened. After a moment of silence, he said, "I saw him take his last breath this morning. He made a loud sound like gasping for air." His voice cracked, and he wept.

"I had no idea he was deteriorating so fast." I felt grateful and indebted to Jun-chan for being there.

"Here's Mom," he said.

When she got on the phone, I said, "Sorry to hear of Dad's passing."

"It was very sudden," she said. "No one could have predicted he'd go this quickly."

I expected her to break down, but her voice sounded surprisingly strong and firm.

"Just two days ago, we all got together for the first time ever in a decade, really a decade, can you believe it? It was so unusual. And we ate dinner together at a restaurant to celebrate the New Year."

By "we all," she meant herself, Jun-chan, Hiro-chan, his wife, their daughter, and the daughter's husband and two kids. Dad would have been too incapacitated to join them. I felt a twinge of sadness to realize something as ordinary as a family get-together was such a special treat to her. They all lived in the same apartment building and yet hardly ever saw each other.

"Two days later, Dad passed," she said. "I can't help thinking he must have had something to do with it. He must have helped make the gathering happen."

"Hmm, maybe." I was skeptical of her usual supernatural way of thinking. "Mom, Jun-chan was crying when I talked to him just now."

"Yeah. He's been crying off and on. He was right beside Dad when he took his last breath."

"I wish I could have been there too," I said.

The last time I'd gone back to Japan was four years ago. That time, my dad had become so sick with a high fever that he almost didn't recover. Since that visit, I'd been preparing myself for the reality that he could go at any time, but his death still shook me.

My mom and I spoke for a few more minutes. Before hanging up, I asked when Dad's funeral would be held and whether I should get a plane ticket. She brushed off my concern and said I didn't have to come back. I wasn't sure if she really meant it or if she was being her passive-aggressive self, and later she'd complain about my absence.

I really didn't want to go back. I imagined the physically and emotionally taxing ordeal of the long flight and the big two-day event—the evening wake of *tsuya* (passing the night) on the first day with a big crowd of mourners, and the *kokubetsushiki* (farewell ceremony) on the second. In addition to enduring the considerable jet lag, there was my near-phobia of flying. Worst of all, going home to Japan meant I'd have to deal with the old, negative family dynamic all over again.

When I expressed my hesitation to Peter, he insisted I attend the funeral. "Buy your ticket now. You have to go." He'd flown back to attend his father's funeral in Minnesota and was grateful he'd done it.

Luckily, I found a reasonably priced ticket, and with my dad's funeral delayed due to a backlog at the crematorium, I arrived in time for the wake.

The *tsuya* was to be held on Saturday evening. My family and several long-term employees of my dad's hospital, including a nurse whom I'd known since I was a child, met at the memorial service hall two hours early to rehearse for the ceremony. The nurse was happy to see me and told me that my dad had worn my red bracelet until his last moment. That made me tear up.

I was mesmerized by the room, which was extensively decorated with elegant floral arrangements along three of the walls, each bearing the name of its sender written on a long, flat wooden board in the center. I walked up to the coffin where my dad lay, looking pristine and peaceful even six days after death. With his emaciated cheeks, he resembled his own father.

"Papa," I said, my eyes filling with tears, my throat closing. Then I shook myself, keeping my tears in check. I couldn't afford to break down yet.

During the rehearsal, one of the coordinators demonstrated the elaborate ritual of the incense offering. Between the shock of my father's death, jet lag, and my hazy menopausal brain, I couldn't quite get it, even after practicing a few times. I grew nervous, worried I might embarrass myself and my family in front of the large crowd. I practiced it again and again with my sister-in-law, Kyoko-san, while repeating the steps out loud. The other funeral coordinators and assistants chuckled as they passed me. No matter how long I'd been away from the culture, I felt I had to fit in and avoid committing a faux pas at all costs.

The *tsuya* began at 6:00 p.m. as soon as the Buddhist priest and two young monks entered the memorial service room and were seated. The priest sat in front of my dad's coffin, which had been placed against the backdrop of white flower arrangements with a large photo of him in the center. Several feet away, on each side of the priest, sat the two monks, facing him. Behind the priest on the right, the ten immediate family members sat in two rows facing the guests in the other half of the room. The monks looked much younger than the ones I was accustomed to seeing at funerals. With shaved heads, clean-shaven faces, and pale, smooth skin, they gave off a fresh and youthful energy.

While the priest was offering *howa* (the Buddhist sermon), my mind wandered. Occasionally, I glanced at the crowd of about two hundred fifty attendees, marveling at how many people had revered my dad. With the limited number of seats available, it was standing room only with mourners flowing out of the room. Among them were several dignitaries: regional politicians, company presidents, representatives from the Rotary Club and Soroptimists, adult Boy Scout and Girl Scout leaders in their uniforms, doctors, nurses, and former patients. Even his barber had come.

At the same time, I was baffled by the disparity between his grand public persona and his private self, the man who had a minimal presence in our family as a father. He'd accomplished so much in his public life. Besides being a great general surgeon who had founded his own hospital, he'd been honored with numerous accolades for his dedication to community service. He had even received two lifetime contribution awards for his philanthropy and public service from the emperor of Japan. But I'd never gotten to know much of his personal side.

He'd never spoken of his past, and I hadn't pried. But even if I had, would he have told me anything? I was hoping to see Mr. Tamura for more information. But unfortunately, he'd contracted a serious case of pneumonia and was too sick to attend the service or even talk on the phone.

I now regretted how little effort I'd made to get to know my father better, especially to hear stories about his childhood. I felt deep sorrow; he'd missed out on life by never experiencing the warmth of a close-knit family. He must have felt terribly lonely and isolated, just as I'd felt growing up in our family. The greatest tragedy of all was that he hadn't known how to connect with us after having extricated himself from the family (a process that, when I think of it, had been happening for most of my life). I was grateful that Peter had been heavily involved in David's life and that they'd formed a close bond.

As the chanting began, each of the immediate family members offered prayers by burning incense. White clouds wafted through the room. The chanting continued for well over two hours until all of the mourners had had a chance to perform the ritual of offering incense to the urn on the altar. In the meantime, the thick smoke enveloped us in a dense, suffocating cloud, making me cough. I stood with my family members in a receiving line toward the exit door to greet and thank each attendee as they left the room. It was a very formal occasion, so we had to bow to each person more deeply than usual. And since each bowed multiple times and we had to bow back in kind, the number of bows easily exceeded a thousand—far more than I was accustomed to doing in one day. After the wake was over, my body was stiff and my neck ached.

The next morning, we returned to the venue around 9:30 a.m. to prepare for the 11:30 a.m. funeral service. My mom, who was still as appearance-conscious as ever in her classy black funeral attire, had approved of my choice of clothes for the first day, but when I showed up at the funeral hall in black slacks, she eyed them with disdain.

"You should have worn yesterday's skirt."

I ignored her.

The crowd of mourners at the *kokubetsushiki* was much smaller, about forty or so, which was quite typical. During the service, the Buddhist priest ceremonially introduced my dad's *kaimyo* (his afterlife Buddhist name written on a small wooden board), consisting of nine kanji. Each bore a noble meaning, such as blessing, joy, service, and virtue. I'd managed to retain my composure throughout the previous day, but then the priest began chanting the *Hannya Shingyo* (the Heart Sutra), along with a simple beat of a *mokugyo* (the fish-shaped wooden drum) to keep up the rhythm: *This body itself is emptiness, and emptiness itself is this body.*

Suddenly tears rolled down my cheeks as I remembered chanting this sutra with Dad. It had been Dad's favorite sutra and had become mine too. Through our shared love of this sutra I felt a deep spiritual connection with him.

The memorial service reached its climax when the pallbearers brought the coffin down from the altar to the center of the room for everyone to have a final look at my father. First, his Boy Scout uniform was laid over his body, and then the funeral coordinators brought us tray after tray heaped with flowers. The flowers had been taken from each of the ninety-eight standing sprays of white flowers: large multilayer chrysanthemums (the traditional funeral flower in Japan), orchids, and Casablanca lilies. The lovely scent of those lilies was no match for the overpowering smell of the constantly burning incense. Each attendee took some of those flowers and placed them around and over my dad's body, except on his face.

My mom laid her palm on my dad's forehead and kept saying in a tearful voice, "Oh, so cold, so cold."

I also placed my hand over his face and whispered, "Papa, Papa."

Jun-chan followed suit, crying.

After my dad's body was completely covered by flowers, the coffin was sealed. My mom and Hiro-chan each gave a short speech, but Hiro-chan broke down and could barely complete his. This was the first time I'd *ever* seen him cry in my entire life. It was so powerful that it made me cry all over again. My nose ran faster than I could contain with sniffles, and with no tissue, I kept using my hand to wipe my nose. Such an oversight not to bring a handkerchief, but a good call not to wear mascara.

It was then time to accompany my dad's coffin to the crematorium. The procession was a private affair, involving only immediate family members, close relatives, and family friends. My mom and I rode together in the large and luxurious black hearse. Before loading the casket into the hearse, ceremony coordinators handed each of us a special item. Mom was given Dad's *kaimyo*. Jun-chan received a wooden box containing a green urn covered with a silvery-white cloth. I received Dad's photo in a royal-blue, velvety frame decorated with several magenta orchid flowers. Jun-chan followed us in his ivory BMW, while Hiro-chan followed with his family in his brand-new Jaguar. A few other cars followed with those who were also participating in the cremation ceremony.

The hearse driver indicated that he would detour to drive by the Ito Hospital, which my dad had founded in 1968. He'd served as the owner and director until ten years ago when he became incapacitated by a massive stroke. Hiro-chan, also a physician, had succeeded him. When we got to the hospital, about thirty nurses, assistants, and helpers were lined up, half on each side of the road.

My mom and I got out of the car, bowed deeply, and said, "Thank you very much for seeing us off."

Many of them had red, puffy eyes. I spotted Maria-san, a kind and gentle Filipino nurse who had been so nice to my dad when he'd been in the nursing home. Her eyes, too, were red and puffy. I looked at her intently for a moment and smiled as a gesture to thank her personally, and she smiled back faintly. Then the hearse resumed its route to the crematorium.

Sitting close to my mom in the back seat with my dad's coffin right behind us, the thought of having to participate in the impending cremation rituals made me cringe. When I was three, I experienced a cremation when my maternal grandfather died. It was held at a shabby, dimly lit facility in a small countryside town on Sado Island. The space was so bare and dingy, it looked like an old factory. The family, relatives, and friends had stood with their heads down, surrounding the chamber in absolute silence while waiting for my grandfather's body to be incinerated. It was quite dark, with only natural light coming through the open door, blurring the figure of each attendee. Luckily, being so little, I was excused from participating in the *kotsuage*, the bone-picking ritual, but I still watched it from behind the adults with my hands partially covering my eyes. The atmosphere had been somber and gloomy, and the ritual so graphic and terrifying, that those images were forever burned into my mind. At age fifty-three, I was no longer afraid but still dreaded having to go through the whole procedure.

The crematorium this time was modern and neat. The white walls, minimalist decor, and spacious high ceilings reminded me of a museum lobby. We followed my dad's coffin as it was carried to the front of the designated chamber. The priest chanted a sutra as we took turns offering incense and prayers before the coffin was loaded into the chamber. An attendant told us to allot approximately seventy minutes for the incineration process before returning. In the meantime, we were escorted to our assigned waiting room with catered sushi and cooked vegetable dishes, as well as the cookies and chocolates we'd brought from home for all of us to share. The main priest and two apprentice monks also joined us.

Then the ominous moment arrived for us to be escorted to the area where my dad's skeletal remains lay on the still-scorching metal plate that had just come out of the chamber. In Japanese cremations, the body is only partially incinerated so that some charred bone fragments are allowed to remain. It was a gruesome scene, with much of his skull and other bones still intact. There were deep sighs, but no one said a word.

We were ushered into a room with milky marble walls and floor. We had to wait there for a good thirty minutes until the remains cooled down enough for the attendant to prepare them on metal trays for our *kotsuage* ceremony. They rattled as he ferried them over on a silver cart. He then instructed us to line up two by two in front of the metal tray filled with the bone fragments and ashes alongside the green ceramic urn. Working in pairs, we were to pick up a single bone together by using long chopsticks (two pairs of chopsticks touching the same piece at the same time) and deposit it inside the urn. My father's bones were carefully arranged so that we could start with the feet and gradually move up to the head. This would ensure that the feet were placed at the bottom of the urn and the remaining parts rested correctly in the upright position (not upside down) inside the urn. I had no idea how everything would manage to fit in there. We repeated this procedure until everyone had at least one chance to pick up a piece of bone.

After what seemed like a very long time, the crematory attendant took over to complete the rest of the procedure. Piece by piece, he transferred the remaining fragments into the urn, describing to us in a calm, quiet voice, "This is a part of his knee," or "This is a part of his elbow," and so on. Everybody nodded with occasional utterances of "Oh" or "Uh-huh." It almost seemed like the attendant was showcasing and appraising precious metals or rare gems.

At one point he stopped and said, "I'm sorry, but his bones are in great shape for a ninety-four-year-old man. May I have your permission to grind them down a bit so that I can make more room in the urn for the rest of them?"

He looked around to make sure no one objected, and then began crushing the bones with a metal rod. A painful grinding sound echoed through the room. It was so graphic some people turned away, but I looked right at it. By this time, the researcher in me had kicked in. *Might as well turn this into an anthropological experience.*

The attendant continued the grinding procedure with a few more bones. When he picked up the only floating bone in the body called the hyoid (located in the neck), he explained that it was the most sacred part of the body. Then he picked up a flat piece of bone. "This is the top of his skull."

I noticed a small hole in it. Kyoko-san stood next to me, slim and delicate, and I touched her forearm. "What do you think that little hole is?"

"I don't know," she whispered, her eyes widened.

The attendant didn't have the answer, but my doctor brother said, "That's from a drainage tube that was inserted when he had a subdural hematoma after he'd suffered a head injury from falling down, remember?"

It was yet another painful reminder of how my dad's health had declined.

After the top of his skull was placed last inside the urn, the attendant swept up the remaining ashes using a mini broom and dustpan, deposited them inside the urn, and closed the lid.

Though I used to fear and be repulsed by the *kotsuage* ceremony, I understood this time how meaningful and effective it was in bringing a sense of closure. I felt closer to my family and deeply appreciated the unity this experience had created.

I knew that taking part in the Japanese funeral—steeped in Buddhist traditional liturgy, rituals, and customs—would be an exhausting ordeal. Still, I tried my best to put our differences aside. We were not much of a family, but I was glad to have returned to participate with them in Dad's funeral. With his passing, my remaining emotional ties to the family died as well. While it was sad, it also brought a liberating sense of resolution.

Family of Victims

January 2015

Late Sunday evening, shortly after returning from dinner, my mom, Kyoko-san, Jun-chan, and I waited for the funeral service director to arrive at Mom's apartment.

"What a funeral that was," I said. "So grandiose and extravagant. It was like a funeral version of Jun-chan's wedding."

Kyoko-san burst out laughing.

"What do you mean?" Jun-chan looked offended. "Is that supposed to be sarcasm?"

I grinned. His wedding reception had been held at one of the fanciest hotels in Tokyo and emceed by a famous TV personality and comedic newscaster. Because Jun-chan was marrying into a Kardashian-like family where the sisters were well-known television celebrities, the guest list was a who's who of celebrities and dignitaries. There was even a formal full-course French meal. It was all so excessive and gaudy, I couldn't even imagine how much it had cost.

I wasn't trying to provoke my brother—or at least not consciously. But I did enjoy teasing him. When he was younger, Jun-chan had been a religious user of a tanning lamp, and his skin tone remained unnaturally dark. I used to call him a Japanese Eddie Murphy. When he was younger, he'd been something of a playboy, always dating gorgeous models and actresses, and while he was still a stylish dresser, his middle-aged belly had put a dent in his reputation with the ladies.

Soon the funeral director came over to help set up the temporary altar to display my dad's urn, photo, and *kaimyo*, along with two large flower arrangements, an incense urn, and ceremonial offerings, such as fancy gift melons and apples. She recommended that each of us light one incense stick twice daily (morning and night) until the forty-ninth day after his death. In Buddhism, the forty-ninth day after death is considered a milestone—the amount of time it takes for the deceased to ascend to Buddhahood. My dad's urn would then be buried at the grave site at Sojiji Temple in Yokohama alongside his ancestors.

"Make sure you eat these food offerings," the director said as she left. "It'll console the deceased."

Then finally, it was over. What a relief. Though, just as quickly, exhaustion set in. Mom, Kyoko-san, and I sat at the kitchen table having some green tea, and Jun-chan rested on the leather couch, parking himself in front of the giant TV.

"It was such a big funeral," Kyoko-san said. "Almost two hundred fifty guests. Does anyone have an estimate of the total cost?"

"Well, let's see," I said. "If you have to pay a million yen (about ten thousand USD) for Dad's *kaimyo* and another million yen to the monks, then wow, there goes two million yen already." The average cost of a funeral in Japan was about 2.5 million yen, so ours must have been way over that.

"Six million yen," my mom said. "The director just told me."

"What!" Kyoko-san and I exclaimed.

I looked at Mom, dismayed. "Why didn't you give the funeral director a budget?" My voice grew louder as my irritation intensified.

"How are we supposed to pay for it?" Kyoko-san shrieked.

I reached over and stroked her back. While I'd always known her to be tough-minded, it was rare for her to speak out like that. She usually came across as quite detached, to the point where Mom and Jun-chan thought her cold. I always thought she was just keeping a wise distance from them.

Kyoko-san and Hiro-chan had a limited budget, and Kyoko-san had been reluctant to have such a large funeral. But Mom had insisted that Dad deserved it. Eventually, Kyoko-san had caved in and allowed Mom to invite as many people as she wanted. It was classic: Mom threw an extravagant event, only to realize later that she couldn't afford it, and then left the rest of the family, principally Hiro-chan and Kyoko-san, scrambling to figure out how to pay for it.

Mom now looked totally ticked off and swaggered in front of us. "We have *koden* (an offering of money) from two hundred fifty people. That should cover most of the cost."

"No," Kyoko-san said, "it's only going to be about 2.5 million yen. That still leaves us 3.5 million short."

"Once I get his life insurance money, I can cover the rest of the cost," Mom said. "I'm expecting eight million yen, so—end of discussion."

"But you won't get the money right away," Kyoko-san said. "It might take quite a while, and we'll still have to pay in the meantime." She sighed deeply. "I feel suddenly exhausted."

"Let's ask Dad to help us out," I said in an effort to lighten the mood. "I think he'll help us in spirit. He must."

"Hmm, I think you're right," Kyoko-san said. "We've gone through so many crises in the past, but every time there has been a silver lining. So yeah, let's stay positive."

It was almost 10:00 p.m., so Kyoko-san said goodnight and left.

Financial anxiety had always been a serious issue in my family.

But it became especially harrowing after Dad embarked on an ambitious business venture to build an eleven-story apartment building during Japan's real estate bubble in the 1980s. The plan was that he and Mom would live on the top floor, each of my brothers would have two floors, and the rest of the building would be reserved for rental units. But Japan's economic collapse starting in the 1990s, along with Dad's stroke, unleashed an avalanche of repercussions, and Mom was forced to file for bankruptcy. To avoid foreclosure, Hiro-chan bought the apartment building for the equivalent of three million USD (a quarter of its original cost), so they were at least able to hold on to it.

As with many family-owned businesses, in which family members are given fabricated executive positions (but don't do any real work) as a way of keeping money in the family, my mom had for decades received a generous monthly salary as the executive director, essentially just for being the wife of the hospital owner and director. And Jun-chan, too, had held a similar type of position. After my dad became incapacitated following his stroke and was removed from the hospital directorship, the family income plummeted when all three were taken off the payroll.

Not only that, but at the time of the bankruptcy, everything came out in the open—the secrecy, mishandlings, and cover-ups. For instance, Jun-chan had secretly been paid the equivalent of half a million USD for his bogus, self-appointed role as a construction supervisor while the family apartment was being built. His business card read, "Ito Property Management CEO," for a company that consisted of only himself. He had also been embezzling some of the tenants' rent payments that he was supposed to be collecting; the totals always came up short.

With Mom and Jun-chan's entire credibility damaged (after the revelation of the things she'd done in cahoots with him), Hiro-chan and Kyoko-san had no choice but to take over the finances, and the responsibility of staying financially vigilant had fallen mainly into Kyoko-san's lap. I was appalled to find this out from Hiro-chan, who'd sent me a lengthy, scathing email. He'd kept it all hidden from me for several years. It was the first time he had ever reached out to me, and I was happy to hear from him even though he was just venting his anger and frustration.

When I had returned to Japan in 1993 to collect data for my dissertation research, I never saw Jun-chan, even though he was supposed to be living in the family's apartment building with his then-wife, Megumi-san—a former beauty queen ten years his junior and a Japanese version of a Kardashian. One day Megumi-san asked me over for tea, which was when I found out they'd been living apart. He'd been married to her for three years, but their marriage had crumbled long before that. He'd been staying at his celebrity friends' places in Tokyo or may already have been living in his luxurious Roppongi Hills apartment while abandoning her and Sapphire, their million-yen (ten-thousand-USD) Scottish Fold cat. I don't know when Megumi-san moved out and officially divorced him, but the two-floor apartment stayed empty for nearly twenty years—save for the cat, which Mom and the housekeeper took turns feeding.

But Mom's financial fallout also caused Jun-chan's downfall, and he had to give up his expensive apartment in Roppongi. That was why he'd moved back into the two-story apartment. When I came home this time, it was jarring to see him hanging out so often at Mom's apartment as it was uncharacteristic of him.

Although I'd always perceived Jun-chan and Mom as two peas in a pod—or rather, two coconspirators who helped bring down the family's finances—I still wanted to stay positive and loving with them. I saw our interactions as opportunities to practice patience and compassion.

That night, after we discussed the cost of the funeral and Kyoko-san left, I thought I'd go to bed. But Jun-chan, who'd been resting on the couch, came over to sit at the kitchen table. I was tired, but it seemed important to stay and keep him and Mom company for a bit.

Since I was holding a rice cracker in my right hand, I poured myself more tea using my left hand.

Mom's eyes popped open. "That's *sakate*!" She yanked the teapot away from me. "No left hand. It's bad luck."

I slumped in my chair. *This again.* Her wild superstitions always came as a surprise after I'd been away from them for a while. I wondered what she would have done if I were left-handed, but I kept that thought to myself, determined to keep things positive.

At first, we talked benignly about the funeral. But I couldn't swallow my concern over the cost.

"You know," I eyed the teapot but kept my left hand in my lap, "Peter is very sensible. I learned from him to become more frugal. He hates to waste anything, but particularly money. He's militantly against paying in installments because he hates paying interest, so we pay off our credit card balances in full every month. We don't live beyond our means, so we have no debts. It keeps our life simple, and we don't have to lose sleep over money concerns."

"Is that right?" Mom said. "That's great to be able to live like that." She made it sound like an idea akin to living on the moon. She always stretched out payments as long as possible, oblivious to the fact that it would cost her more in the long run. She never believed in the importance of saving money.

Jun-chan remained silent. Last I heard he was running from loan sharks. I didn't mean to lecture him for having lived his life doing exactly the opposite, but it occurred to me that I might have hit a nerve. I wanted to help him, but in retrospect, I chose the worst moment to do it.

In the tatami room where I slept, there were a few dozen shopping bags full of Jun-chan's personal belongings. Among them were many empty Louis Vuitton boxes and paper shopping bags sitting exactly where he'd left them a year ago when he'd been waiting to move back into his own apartment three floors down. Many of his clothes, including slacks, coats, and leather jackets, were still covered by dry cleaners' plastic bags and hung across the railing above the sliding *shoji* screen doors. It was suffocating, and Mom had complained that his stuff had been sitting there for too long and that she was tired of it taking up so much space. But even more than that, it wasn't a good way to live.

"Jun-chan," I said, "you need to do some feng shui and declutter your stuff so that you can let more positive things come into your life, including money." I was the last person who should be giving advice on the art of decluttering. But having implemented it myself, I'd seen some positive results. I felt emotionally lighter and had an easier time prioritizing things. I was convinced this practice would benefit him too.

"Shut the fuck up!" he yelled. "I know that already. No one's ever pissed me off this much. Ever!"

For a moment, I was speechless. *I don't know who this person is anymore.* But then I blurted, "Why get so mad? I didn't come home to get into a fight with you. I simply wanted to help you. But I don't care anymore. You do whatever you want."

He got up abruptly and stomped out. Several seconds later, the front door slammed.

We'd never fought like this before. I had no idea how my feng shui advice could have triggered such a reaction. "He sounded like a mobster," I muttered.

"He explodes so easily," Mom said. "He must have thought we were ganging up on him because I've been nagging him about that too. He's been under a lot of pressure."

"Well, tough shit. He deserves it," I said. "What goes around, comes around. Besides, he moved back here a year ago, and if he hasn't touched any of that stuff, he probably doesn't need it." I understood how daunting it must have been for him to pick up the pieces of his life, but he had to start somewhere.

Mom only looked more concerned. "He's really *fubin*, you know." (A poor thing.) "I feel so sorry for him. He must be feeling awful, hitting a dead end in every direction."

I'd heard this a million times. Mom thought Jun-chan had been mistreated, never having received his fair share within our family. She argued he was such a good-natured guy, which made him easy prey for scammers. But as far as I knew, he'd been given every opportunity he'd asked for. He was the one who never followed through, whether it was dental school, real estate school, opening a fancy restaurant in Tokyo, or getting involved in a series of get-rich-quick schemes, like selling two-hundred-dollar shampoo. My parents had invested in him every time, only to have him squander everything.

"If only we'd had enough money to send him to medical school when he wanted to go." Mom's voice was whiny.

Please. It was moments like these when I felt like slapping her. "Mom, wake up. Even if he'd been lucky enough to get into medical school, he would have dropped out."

For her to have repeatedly bailed him out to spare him the pain of standing on his own two feet had done him a great disservice. This "poor Jun-chan" mentality had kept him from learning how to become an independent adult. No matter how many times or how terribly Jun-chan deceived us or betrayed our trust, Mom always gave him the benefit of the doubt, trusting that he would someday turn himself around. The rest of us, though, had given up on him a long time ago.

"He must have been feeling terribly distressed. When he doesn't come up here to visit me for several days, I worry that he's committed suicide," Mom said.

I scoffed. "If he had enough courage to kill himself, he would have turned his life around a long time ago. He's almost sixty, and he's done nothing except accumulate debts."

Mom was no longer listening, or rather, she was unwilling to listen to me anymore. She adamantly held on to this ridiculous victimhood narrative. I stood up, ending our discussion. It was a waste of time and energy.

But I felt bad for having quarreled with Jun-chan. I hadn't meant to upset him. I thought about calling him to apologize. But when I called Kyoko-san for advice, she suggested that I allow a cooling-off period at least till the next morning, for he would likely be too upset now to listen to me.

I finally retreated to the tatami room, overcome by physical and emotional exhaustion. I felt like screaming. This was making me crazy. Nothing would ever change in this family. I had to get out of there.

The next morning, there was nothing good to eat for breakfast—not even rice—because, as usual, Mom didn't feel like cooking. I told her I'd just graze on snack food, but a few minutes later she grabbed her purse and hurried to the front door.

"Where are you going?" I asked.

"To the deli across the street to get some *onigiri* for Jun-chan."

Some rice balls. "I don't want him to get upset again that there's nothing decent to eat in the house."

I was stunned. "Mom! He's an adult. He can go get it himself if he wants. You're treating him like a little child." Just as I was about to add that my seventeen-year-old son was more independent than that, she left.

Is he really, though? I realized I was in no position to lecture her. Wasn't I just as guilty of coddling David?

When I'd first arrived back in Japan, I was grateful to have the opportunity to get to know Jun-chan better now that we were both middle-aged adults. But being around him and my mom had become more wearing than the funeral. As the trip dragged on, fatigue set in from the jet lag, sleep deprivation, and perhaps menopause as well. I became snappier and increasingly critical, and the rest of our time together didn't go well. I was disappointed, but not surprised, by how easily my positive feelings had evaporated.

On the day I was flying back to Seattle, Kyoko-san, who'd been working full-time as the chief pharmacist at Ito Hospital, took the morning off to drive me to the airport shuttle bus station. She was the only person in the family with whom I could talk about things openly.

I'd known Kyoko-san since I was in middle school when she was dating my brother Hiro-chan. I'd always been fond of her, admired her beauty, and looked up to her like an older sister for her intelligence, levelheadedness, and inner strength. Her soft, feminine exterior belied a tough and stoic personality. Her marriage to Hiro-chan for over thirty-four years had endured many rough patches, not surprisingly correlating with the never-ending cycle of the Ito family's financial woes. But she'd persevered, and things had started looking up.

As we drove out of the garage, my mom waited outside with a pensive look on her face. I rolled down the window, shook hands with her, and said matter-of-factly, "Bye, Mom, I'll call you when I get home. You take care, okay?"

I closed the window.

"She looks like she wants to come along," said Kyoko-san. "Don't you think we should invite her?"

"No, it's okay," I said. "I already told her she doesn't have to come." In truth, I was looking forward to catching up with Kyoko-san and restoring normalcy after spending so much time with Mom and Jun-chan.

"Oh, but look." Kyoko-san pointed. Mom was crying.

"She's a drama queen. She'd just cry again at the bus station. I don't have the energy to deal with that."

As my mother became smaller in the rearview mirror, I felt a twinge of guilt. I was happy to leave, but she was obviously feeling sad. I didn't have much respect for her, but I did care about her. I stuck my head out the window and waved one last time, then sank into the seat and breathed a deep sigh of relief.

"I can't believe I was only here for five days," I said. "It seemed more like three weeks." I felt a rush of gratitude that I had a home in Seattle to return to and that my family there was where my heart really belonged. We'd been through a tough year and a half, but compared to this, our situation suddenly seemed less serious.

And yet, something nagged at me. There was something about Mom's learned helplessness, her victim narrative, and codependency with Jun-chan that made me uncomfortable. What if I was becoming more like her? My relationship with David wasn't all that different from hers with Jun-chan. It occurred to me that I was just as guilty of blaming other people or situations for my problems and evading responsibility to get my act together.

But these were terribly disheartening thoughts, so I turned back to Kyoko-san and gossiped about our Japanese family instead.

Cold Turkey

March 2015 to November 2015

On a Saturday afternoon in March, about two months after my father's funeral, I was reading in my study while David and Liz were engaged in a solemn conversation in the kitchen. Their tone made me curious, but I resisted the temptation to eavesdrop. When Liz started to weep, I felt uneasy and thought about checking on them but stayed away. I didn't want to meddle.

After the front door slammed shut, I made my way warily down to the kitchen. David sat on a stool by the island, his gaze pensive.

"I broke up with Liz," he said.

I was shocked. They'd been together for nearly two years. There'd been no sign of trouble as far as I could tell.

"I didn't have to do it!" he shouted, and soon tears rolled down his cheeks. He said he didn't want to hurt her and could have stayed with her even though he no longer loved her.

I hugged him while he cried himself out. As heartbreaking as it was to see him this way, I was relieved. I wouldn't have to worry about them attending the same college and tying the knot. No more hosting a weekend bed-and-breakfast.

David didn't immediately elaborate on the reason for their breakup, but days later he told me he'd started to fall out of love around eight months earlier. While Liz's sensitivity had helped him get in touch with his emotions, and her passion and discipline toward music had been critical in furthering his musicality, he'd felt suffocated by her overreliance on him and had become unhappy. He also missed his interactions with his school friends. His sense of obligation to her could only last for so long. I was glad he'd come to this conclusion on his own.

Shortly after, we had a family session with David's college counselor at his high school. She fully supported his choice of colleges with strong music programs but warned us that his application process would be more grueling than that of his classmates because of the additional audition requirements. Despite some reservations, Peter and I supported his ambition to pursue a dual degree in music and academics.

Although I knew that the college admission hysteria would continue for another nine months or even a year if his early action application didn't succeed, at least the relationship saga was over. I felt so relieved and lighthearted that I quit—cold turkey—the daily Venlafaxine I'd been taking for several years to alleviate my hot flashes, night sweats, and other menopause-related symptoms. Why should I bother consulting any doctors when I thought it was no big deal? The medication didn't seem to be helping much. I hadn't felt like myself for months, with more pronounced fatigue, disorienting brain fog, and headaches. I figured these were menopausal symptoms that I simply had to endure and didn't realize the medication had also been taking the edge off of other underlying symptoms.

A couple of weeks later, David showed me a photo of a girl named

Ana, who he'd met through a mutual friend and was planning to ask to the upcoming school dance.

"Another cellist," he said. "Don't you think she's pretty?"

Not again. "Well, yeah, but you just broke up with Liz. Shouldn't you have a moratorium on dating for a while?"

"No worries, Mom. It'll just be platonic."

I sighed, resigned, and made no further comment.

Soon they began dating in earnest. Ana was a petite girl with big, brown, sparkly eyes. Her parents were Russian-Jewish immigrants who had fled Russia and then hopscotched across the Middle East and Europe before landing in America.

When Ana and I met after the dance, the first thing that came out of her mouth was, "Oh, you're so beautiful!"

I was taken aback and felt a bit awkward, but her flattery lifted my spirits. Although I habitually dismissed similar compliments from Peter, hers somehow had more impact. Whether it was genuine or not, she was a much-needed cheerleader for my self-esteem. She came across as direct and self-assured with a contagious, bubbly personality. I liked her instantly.

Before long, she started telling me she loved me at every opportunity. It was baffling, and at first, I wasn't sure how to respond. This was neither something people said casually in my Japanese culture nor in our stoic Seattle household. But it soon became a second-nature interaction with her, as if she were nudging me to become more effervescent and expressive. We also exchanged hugs routinely. Looking back, I can see it was a sign of neediness. She was trying to ingratiate herself with me, perhaps hoping I'd welcome her into our family. But at the time, I didn't detect anything amiss about her fun-loving and exuberant behavior, at least for the first few months. I'd grown tired of my tendency to be suspicious and must have let my guard down.

In late spring, when Peter's brother George flew in to visit us from Minnesota, I asked David to pick him up from the airport. He took the dented and scratched Honda.

As Peter and I were helping George settle into our guestroom, he mentioned he'd spotted a sleeping bag, blankets, and pillows in the back seat and asked us facetiously if David liked camping in his car. Peter laughed it off, but I blushed. I didn't know whether it was appropriate for David to be having routine car sex with Ana. Over time, though, their steamy relationship became a source of concern. Were they practicing safe sex? I wasn't sure how to bring it up. I had attended a Christian girls' school in Japan, where sex had been a foreign concept. It hadn't been much of a concern while David was dating Liz because, according to him, her physical condition and depression made her uninterested in sex. When I mentioned it to Peter, he didn't seem worried at all. He trusted David to practice safe sex even though they'd never discussed it.

The period of several weeks in midsummer while David attended the Interlochen Arts Camp in Michigan was a welcome respite. But when Ana told me her usual cello practice space had become unavailable and that she couldn't practice at home because her mother operated a medical group home there, I offered our home to her for practice several hours each day while David was gone. Though I wasn't too impressed by her cello playing and thought Liz had been more disciplined and a much better cellist, Ana appeared to be dedicated enough and was aiming for Juilliard, so I was all in to support her endeavors. She'd come to me after practice to show me the calluses she'd developed on her fingers, saying that she had to show them to her cello teacher as evidence of her efforts. I winced at the sight of the red, painful-looking lumps.

As for David, the music camp turned out to be a disappointment;

it was designed more for orchestra students and not set up well for piano students. He had to navigate the learning mostly on his own. He sounded dispirited, though not to the extent he'd been at his first music camp two summers before. I became rattled again, wondering how he would survive the six-week-long camp.

In the meantime, Peter must have thought this was an opportune time to recharge our sex-starved marriage. After David's call, I went into the bedroom and found a silver lipstick vibrator sitting on my pillow. This overt gesture enraged me so much that I threw it across the room. *Is this all he can think about?* A couple of hours later, before he could make any advances, I told him I had a headache. It wasn't a lie, but I exaggerated, saying that it was splitting and that I needed to take Aleve and go to bed early. His eyes dimmed with disappointment and sadness or perhaps pent-up frustration and desperation.

"I can't keep living like this," he shouted, stomping into his office and shutting the door.

I felt a twinge of guilt but shook it off. The minor headache I had earlier started to throb, and I did indeed have to take an Aleve and lie down.

After that, Peter rarely initiated sex. It should have worried me, but his disappointment and frustration were the last things on my mind. I was overwhelmed by other concerns, not to mention my debilitating menopausal symptoms.

When David returned from music camp, his intense dating with Ana resumed, and they were together whenever possible. Ana ceased practicing her cello altogether, though I stopped short of asking her why because I didn't want to meddle. Then one evening in late August, she got into a heated argument with her mother, who threw a toaster oven at her and then threw her out of the house. We were suddenly scrambling to rescue her. David brought her to our house, fearing for her safety. Surprisingly, Ana remained strong and unfazed, and she didn't shed a single tear. I felt sympathy for her and didn't mind her staying with us for the time being.

The next day when we went back to help her retrieve her belongings, I was shocked to see that her mother had stuffed her things into plastic bags and left them outside. I couldn't believe any mother would do that to her child.

Although Ana said she was relatively close to her divorced father, he was unreliable and had some serious financial issues. Having filed for bankruptcy and currently sharing a small apartment with a roommate, he couldn't provide her with a place to live. As a result, we offered to house her until she could find an apartment. Still, I couldn't relax while she stayed in the house. Anxiety crept up on me by the day. Ana's future was full of uncertainty.

One day when emptying out the wastebasket in David's room, I found a box of king-size condoms along with a K-Y Jelly lubricant box.

I showed the box to Peter when he returned from work, and he snickered. "That's way too big for him. It'll slide right off."

"You've got to confront David about this." I was terrified he would get Ana pregnant.

"No way," Peter said. "It's too awkward."

Peter and I couldn't even discuss our sexless marriage without getting angry at each other. We hadn't talked about it since the last time it had come up in family counseling. It was the elephant in the room that I wished would just disappear. There was no way we could bring up such a touchy subject with our son.

Now that Ana had moved in, Peter and I were committed to

supporting her in any way we could. She needed help, and we'd come to care about her. For a couple of nights we huddled around the kitchen table, discussing logistics and a step-by-step course of action for her to move forward. Peter wrote down the bullet points on a clipboard, and I pitched in with concrete suggestions. These brainstorming sessions were quite militaristic.

Peter put her in contact with his older sister, who'd come a long way since her brief stint in prison for selling drugs. She'd become a clinical psychologist and had helped hundreds of women through her volunteer work with Narcotics Anonymous and domestic violence and abuse women's shelters, for which she'd even received a presidential pardon from George W. Bush. She knew a lot about food stamps and how to enroll in emergency cash distribution programs.

We also encouraged Ana to start looking for a place to live. Initially, she seemed to make progress while we provided moral support and guidance with her job search. Soon, she landed a job at a Boys & Girls Club. We even lent her a thousand dollars as start-up money. Peter stressed that it was not a gift and wrote up a repayment schedule, where she should pay back $25.00 per week, but as a contract, it was hardly enforceable.

One evening in late October, I suggested to Peter that we take Ana and David out to Buca di Beppo, a lively Italian restaurant, to cheer her up. We arrived in a good mood, and the restaurant's red-checkered tablecloths and pictures on the walls gave it a homey feel. After starting with fried calamari, bruschetta, and Caesar salad, we indulged in lasagna and chicken rigatoni. Throughout dinner, we kept our conversation light, talking about music and the kids' future ambitions. We were all grateful to have a moment to decompress.

Ana leaned on David's shoulder to show him her favorite Vines video on her phone, featuring a hilarious Japanese guy. As they were laughing, Peter took a peek at it and laughed with them.

Suddenly, their nonchalance ticked me off. *Does she realize how serious her situation is? Does David?* I couldn't tell whether she was putting on a perky facade to conceal her anxiety or if she simply lacked awareness of the mess she was in. And Peter's Good Samaritan attitude had started to wear on me. Maybe I was finally getting in touch with my repressed feelings of anger and resentment for being dragged into this mayhem. Whatever the cause, I vented my frustration by bringing up an entirely different subject.

"By the way, David, I was sorting through your trash and found an empty box of king-size condoms. Dad said they're way too big for you. They'll slide right off," I said.

I admit it was wildly inappropriate, but Ana was around all the time. I'd come to treat her as family and had grown less concerned about her perception of me. Besides, it felt great to blow off some steam.

Everyone at the table looked dumbfounded. But then David quipped, "Oh no, Mom, I've got a good gene, thanks to Dad."

"How do you know Dad's size? Have you seen it? He's built like a horse," I said with a deadpan expression, placing my hands about shoulder-width apart.

Peter's face flushed bright red. "Shigeko, stop!" He waved his hand in front of my face to shush me.

I ignored him, instead imitating Robert De Niro's signature two-finger *I'm watching you* gesture from *Meet the Parents*. After that, we were less talkative. I had ruined the dinner.

From then on, David fell into the habit of taking his trash can with him whenever he drove anywhere.

Within a day or two, Ana learned that her close friend, Mikhail, had suffered a similar fate with his own volatile, abusive mother, and was looking to move out of her house in the nearby San Juan Islands. Ana decided they should team up and find a place together. David preemptively informed me that Mikhail had been a successful entrepreneur who'd made tons of money by managing a business that operated like a private-jet version of Uber.

When Mikhail came over to our house, we stood in the front hallway for a while as he told us the details of his troubled home situation. He looked like a stereotypical computer nerd, slightly chubby, with a round face, short, curly hair, and Harry Potter-style glasses. There was something about him that made us all look at him with awe as if he were a genius or savior.

"I have seventy thousand USD in my bank account, but I really don't want to touch it unless I absolutely have to. Let me consult my lawyer," Mikhail said.

"Whoa, you have your own lawyer?" I asked.

He nodded.

He was only two years older than David but came across as a very mature young man with a degree of affectation. I wondered if his stilted speech and odd vocabulary were indications of high intelligence or if he was trying a little too hard to exude confidence and maturity—or both. Whenever he discussed money issues, he always specified the amount in US dollars. He claimed to know four programming languages, so he'd have no trouble finding a job. He seemed eccentric, but at least we wouldn't have to worry about him financially—or so we hoped.

David went apartment hunting with them for several days, and when they finally found a studio apartment in Seattle's University District, they asked if we would act as cosigners since their parents refused to get involved. We discussed this for a few days, and at one point Ana offered to put her car up as collateral for her portion of the lease. Even though we hardly knew Mikhail, we finally agreed. He and Ana were extremely grateful for our generosity and promised not to betray our trust.

At this point, I'd been off the Venlafaxine for several months and felt as if my neural circuits were going haywire. I'm not sure whether that was the cause of my backslide, but once again, I became totally blind to the fact that David's life had become my life, and it was unhealthy for our family dynamics.

When David asked if he could move in with his friends, at least Peter and I were clearheaded enough to say, "Absolutely not." What a rare moment of unity. We told him Ana and Mikhail were moving into the apartment because they weren't welcome in their family homes but that he did have a place in his home. Also, he was still in high school, and it was inappropriate for him to move out. Besides, it would be impractical: three people sharing a studio apartment in a crowded neighborhood on the other side of town where he wouldn't even be able to park a car, let alone get himself to school. He couldn't get himself to school on time from two miles away. *What was he thinking?*

Within two weeks, Ana quit her job at the Boys & Girls Club. Of course we were disappointed. How was she going to pay her rent—and repay her loan to us? Within another few weeks, her living arrangement with Mikhail deteriorated, and they came to despise each other.

As if we were their surrogate parents, they turned to us to complain about who had done what. One afternoon Mikhail called to say how enraged he was each time Ana kicked him out when David came to visit. He also railed that the screaming and shouting she made while having sex disturbed the other tenants, putting the two of them at risk of eviction.

"She's so selfish and irresponsible," he said. "I can't stand her anymore."

The next day, Ana came over and, within five minutes, started complaining about Mikhail. "He's such a snitch and a manipulator. I swear, he's a pathological liar."

We didn't know who to believe anymore. Probably neither of them. Peter and I remained sympathetic for a while because they both came from such dysfunctional families. But we also had our limits. It was obvious that they'd hardly known each other and were definitely not the close friends Ana had originally claimed.

Not long after, Ana's mother let her move back in, and she left the apartment. We figured that was it and we'd be on the hook for the rest of the lease, but Mikhail turned out to be as responsible as he initially seemed when we met him. He said he didn't want to betray our trust and generosity and that he would do everything in his power to hold up his end of the deal. He then convinced his mother to pitch in part of the rent at least until the six-month lease expired. We were off the hook for now but still couldn't rest easy until the lease was up.

One November night, reeling from the Ana fallout and fed up with all the craziness, I started ranting. Peter and I were lying in bed. The lights were off because he was trying to sleep, but that didn't stop me.

"This is so crazy. And we were so naive to trust Ana when we hardly knew her. Lending her money was a big mistake. She's a lost cause, and we're never gonna get our thousand dollars back. We have no common sense. So stupid." I said "we," but what I really meant was Peter. It was all his fault. I knew I was pestering him, but once I started, words just kept pouring out of my mouth, and then—

"Stop! Just *stop*!" Peter yelled so loudly that his voice cracked.

I was so surprised I jumped.

"You just keep pushing and pushing and pushing. And you don't know when to stop. I don't want to hear about this anymore. Just let me go to sleep."

I shut down. I couldn't remember the last time he'd flown into a rage like this. I took it as a warning sign. Clearly, his anger toward me had been festering for a long time.

After that, I tried to focus on the one upside to this fiasco: David's gratitude upon finally recognizing the relative normalcy and stability in our family. I was mad as hell at him for dragging us into this but gave him a pass when he acknowledged that his home situation was pretty good. In the midst of the whirlwind, he even managed to file an early action application to Yale.

While all this drama continued to unfold, Ana was clearly latching onto David. One day, I found papers on which she had doodled "Mrs. Ana Anderson." David had mentioned that she wanted an infinity ring for Christmas. Considering how sexually active they seemed, I was afraid she might try to get pregnant on purpose to trap him and ruin his life.

I couldn't think straight. I was having wild mood swings, and the intensity of my hot flashes had increased dramatically. In addition, there were the ever-intensifying college admission anxiety and the growing rift with Peter. It was too much. I was a nervous wreck, lost my appetite, and couldn't relax.

A friend who was a marijuana connoisseur suggested I try a CBD tincture. I was so desperate that I quelled my apprehensions about side effects and headed to Aurora Avenue, where dispensaries were more ubiquitous than Starbucks. I picked one at random, showed my driver's license to the security guard, and stepped inside. I was impressed by how clean and organized it was, with everything displayed in glass cabinets like a fancy chocolate store. The staff made me feel at ease and was knowledgeable enough to answer my questions. I bought a tincture that was supposed to help me relax, along with a CBD cream for my chronic arthritis pain.

I was on cloud nine. I was about to take a potion that would produce a nirvana-like state of relaxation. I took a dose and lay in bed, waiting for the magic to kick in. After about an hour, nothing seemed to be happening. So, I took another dose. Still nothing. After a couple hours, I got bored, so I decided to go grocery shopping at Central Market, a five-minute drive away. As soon as I got there, I felt a little strange, but I continued shopping. Then suddenly, while standing in front of their Big Board Buy section, my whole body felt heavy, my knees locked, and I was momentarily unable to walk. I felt dizzy, my heart palpitated, and I was terrified that I might collapse onto the floor. I stood there for a few minutes until the wave of terror subsided, then checked out quickly before walking to my car.

I managed to drive home but had to lie down until the terrifying sensations subsided. I discarded the tincture right away, swearing never to take it again.

Once I sobered up, I felt a strong urge to get away. It seemed like the only thing that could save my sanity. While I'd never associated my home in Japan as a go-to place for a vacation, the idea of going back there made sense to my racing mind. I'd come home from my father's funeral in January feeling empowered, having gained confidence and a sense of achievement after participating in the elaborate funeral rituals. *Nowhere can be more stressful than here.* I figured I could withstand anything Mom might sling my way.

Maybe the combination of stress and menopause had impaired my ability to make decisions. Clearly, I'd already forgotten how stressful it had been there last time. Or, more likely, my impulsive decision simply reflected the degree of my desperation.

When I called my mother in Japan, she mentioned that the Buddhist ceremony to mark *isshuki*, the first anniversary of my dad's death, was coming up. She had decided to schedule it two months earlier in November, so it would be timely for me to come home. I decided to stay for three weeks. It would mean getting away from the intense situation at home, participating in the ceremony to show family support, eating tons of yummy food, and visiting school shrines to pray for David's college admissions success. I was hopeful that the excruciating admissions process would end in December when he was accepted to Yale.

My dad's *isshuki* ceremony would provide the perfect camouflage for the main objective of this trip: escape.

Minamino Heart Clinic

November 28, 2015

Mom sat at the kitchen table, painting her fingernails with her favorite, muted, pink-beige nail polish. When she finished, she reached for a makeup primer and concealer. For the next half-hour I watched her apply foundation and powder, brush tea-rose blush on her cheeks, and apply her signature Dior red lipstick, first outlining her lips, then filling them in with her lip brush. It took extra time to complete this final step because, to save money, she was squeezing out the last bits from the tube. Finally, she blotted her lips with a tissue and examined herself in the mirror.

"All you're doing is going to the heart clinic," I said. "What's the point of wearing all that makeup?"

She gave me a withering glance as if it was obvious that she couldn't go anywhere without makeup. Public appearance was everything to her. She often told people we were doing just fine when, in fact, we were all terribly estranged, and her life had been falling apart ever since my dad's first major stroke a decade earlier.

Dad had been gone for ten months, and my mother had spiraled into depression, causing herself intense anguish and misery and jeopardizing her own health. In the week since I'd returned her mood had vacillated between self-pity and anger.

"I'll die *kodokushi* (alone, uncared for, and unmourned)," she lamented one day. Last night, she'd snapped with anger. "I'm not expecting you kids to throw me a fancy funeral."

I knew she was fishing for reassurance that we would do exactly that. Instead, I said, "You know, Peter's dad was against a fancy funeral. He insisted on being cremated and having his ashes put in the columbarium at his church." I kept going, knowing it would irritate her. "He was very pragmatic and eco-conscious. It's quite trendy now to scatter ashes into the ocean."

"I hate the ocean," she spat. "I don't even know how to swim."

You asked for it. It was my first thought, but then I felt bad about what I'd said. I always said one thing too many when I should have just kept my mouth shut.

Later that night, I found out she still hadn't had Hiro-chan sign the medical consent form for a possible procedure she might require the next day. I had urged her many times to just call and ask him for it, but she wouldn't, so I finally called him on her behalf. When he came up to her apartment (just one floor above his), Mom bowed obsequiously and said, "I'm very sorry to trouble you." He nodded, signed the form, and then left. I was shocked and pained to see such an estranged interaction between them. After all these years, she was still afraid of him. I felt inexplicable sadness for her and regretted my earlier meanness.

After having ten days of ups and downs, I desperately needed to de-stress. Three weeks prior to my arrival in Japan, I'd scheduled a lunch date with Yukiko and Satomi, two of my best friends from high school who I hadn't seen for years. But the lunch date happened to be on the same day as my mom's medical appointment. It would have been tough to reschedule our get-together, so Mom had insisted I go. Her friend Nishi-san agreed to accompany her to the appointment.

A little after 4:00 p.m., I arrived to meet my mom and Nishi-san at the Minamino Heart Clinic. It was such a windy day that my wool overcoat kept flapping while I walked from the train station to the clinic, my stomach churning with apprehension. My mother was eighty-three. I was afraid to hear what her cardiologist had found. Gingerly, I slid the door open and peeked inside. She lay in the bed looking dazed, her right arm wrapped in bandages and an IV in her left arm.

I'd also asked Jun-chan to come and be with our mother, and he'd agreed to be here by 1:00 p.m., but he was not around. However, Nishi-san sat in a chair, leaning toward my mom's bed and gazing at her with a gentle smile.

Nishi-san was also eighty-three, but unlike my mom, she had remained active and traveled everywhere by train and on foot. They'd known each other through decades of volunteering for Girl Scouts in Yokohama as leaders and later as administrators. Nishi-san had been there with my mom since 10:00 a.m., and I felt indebted to her for her kindness and generosity.

I bowed, saying, "I wished I could have been here sooner." I dug into my purse for the bag of eel crackers one of my friends had given me at lunch. She worked in Hamamatsu, which was famous for its eel production. The plastic bag crinkled as I pulled it out. "You must be hungry. Would you eat these? If you like them, I'd like you to have them."

Her eyes widened. "I'd love that. Thank you." She took the bag with her wrinkled hands, darkened with age spots.

My mom looked limp and spaced out, her mouth slack, so frail in the hospital bed. Nishi-san was studying the ingredient list on the package. "Hmm, rich in calcium," she murmured.

"My mother's condition seems serious," I said. "It wasn't just an exam, was it?"

"I don't know all the details," Nishi-san said with a slight frown. "She underwent some procedure."

My stomach fluttered. Just six months ago, she'd had two stents inserted in her heart. "Where's my brother?"

"He called and said there was too much traffic for him to drive here."

Jun-chan. I had hoped he wouldn't disappoint me, but I should have known better. "That's ridiculous. He could have used the train and been here in less than thirty minutes." Although imagining him deigning to use the train was a whole separate issue. I shook my head in disgust. "I can't count on him for anything."

Nishi-san looked surprised by my intense reaction, but I didn't bother to hide it. It was the same old scenario: my unreliable, self-centered brother evading responsibility yet again. My anger and frustration toward him reignited the fury I'd felt during our phone conversation the night before.

"I don't know where that clinic is. I don't know how to get there," he'd said, cold and detached.

I'd spelled out the address and phone number as though he was a child. "She's your mother, for crying out loud," I'd shouted, and hung up the phone.

He still leeched off our mother. Just a few years earlier he'd hit a new low: after running out of my mom's expensive jewelry to pawn, he'd gone after her social security money to make the lease payments on his top-of-the-line BMW. And now he couldn't be bothered to show up here.

About thirty minutes into my chat with Nishi-san, my mom's cardiologist appeared. Dr. Nakamura was in his early to mid-forties and very handsome. His tanned face and light-brown hair gave him the look of a surfer. I couldn't tell if it was his real hair color or dyed. I guessed he was mixed race.

He asked us to follow him to the nurses' station so that he could show us my mother's X-rays queued up on the computer screen. I helped my mom get up and rolled her IV pole alongside her. On the screen, her heart X-rays were displayed side by side, the one with two stents from the earlier procedure on the left and the other with the newly replaced stents plus one balloon from that day.

"You're lucky your heart problems were detected back in May," he said to my mom. He pointed at one of the two stents and said it had been getting clogged up again, so he'd inserted a new one and performed a dilation in another area.

"This is a lifestyle disease, you know," he said, "so she needs to improve her diet and exercise regularly." He sounded serious and spoke around my mother as if he didn't trust her to listen to him. He'd been her doctor for a while. He must have known she reacted to anything unpleasant by tuning it out.

I told the doctor that my mother was a finicky eater and had strong likes and dislikes. After my dad's passing, she had no appetite for regular food, so she just ate cake every day.

The doctor crossed his arms, looking pensive. "Since you're here, I'd better tell you this. Back in May, when I inserted those two stents, your mother insisted on being discharged the next morning to receive an award at a Soroptimist ceremony." The doctor frowned. "I asked her, 'Which is more important: your life or the award?' But she wouldn't listen, so I made her sign a waiver stating that she was leaving against medical advice."

"Talk about recklessness," I snorted.

My mom looked away and kept quiet.

From time to time, I'd expressed my resentment and frustration toward my mom to people I knew well. But I'd never directly expressed disapproval like this in front of my mother or in front of someone I'd just met. I was surprised by how it all came out of me. But after ten days, I was fed up with her negativity, pessimism, and fatalistic attitude. The fatigue of jet lag only exacerbated my menopausal irritability.

"I'm sorry she hasn't been a good patient," I said to the doctor. It was awkward for me to apologize on her behalf, as though I were at a parent-teacher conference feeling bad for my child's misbehavior. My face felt hot with embarrassment. The role of adult authority had suddenly fallen into my lap, and I felt the urge to somehow make up for my mother's behavior. Neither of my older brothers was any help, nor was Mom willing to take care of herself.

Toward the end of this discussion, the computer screen suddenly switched from X-rays to a picture of two men in black tuxedos and top hats. They looked like showbiz entertainers. *Why are they on the screen saver?*

"Is one of those men you, Doctor?" I blurted.

Everyone around burst into laughter.

Dr. Nakamura maintained a poker face and said, "The one on the right is me."

"That's what I thought." I pointed at the picture, saying, "You're *ikemen* (handsome)."

He shook his head and made a waving hand gesture, indicating he was just kidding. Then he pivoted, an impish grin spreading over his face as he said, "Boy, you are *so* good at flattery."

Throughout this interaction the staff behind us laughed. Both my mom and Nishi-san were laughing too. It was an honest question that had turned into accidental comic relief. After such a serious medical discussion, it lightened the atmosphere and eased the heavy weight on my heart.

Nishi-san went home after the meeting was over, and I was left alone with my mother in the small private hospital room. I felt awkward as usual. We'd spent so much time apart and had never had a good relationship to start with. I never knew what to talk about with her. At least in her apartment, the giant TV was constantly on, blasting news and allowing us to avoid interaction. There was a TV in the hospital room, but it was small and got very few channels. I stood by the window, searching for something to say.

Outside, the orange evening glow was dimming, and a tall, dense evergreen, perfectly shaped like a Christmas tree, became shadow art. I gazed at the scenery for a time and decided I'd leave as soon as my mom finished her dinner.

"Chako-chan, would you get me my blood pressure medicine?" my mom asked.

As soon as I opened the locker where she kept her purse, the smell of Jo Malone's Osmanthus Blossom perfume wafted toward me. It was the perfume I'd given her when I'd returned to Japan for my dad's funeral in January. I was glad she liked it so much, but I felt a strange sadness to be reminded once again of her lifelong preoccupation with public persona.

I stepped out of the room to call Jun-chan. I explained to him that Mom had needed a procedure after all and that the doctor urged her to improve her diet and start exercising—or else.

"There's no way she'll change," he said. "She loves all those unhealthy foods."

"Well, it's doctor's orders. I'll see what I can do while I'm here. But I'm leaving soon, so you'll have to help her. You two often go out to eat, so remind her to eat healthy."

I waited for him to agree, but he said nothing.

"By the way, I spoke to Takeda-san and he agreed to pick her up tomorrow morning at nine. You're off the hook. You must be relieved," I said sarcastically and hung up. Takeda-san worked at Ito Hospital and had additional miscellaneous jobs, including acting as the family handyman and my mom's chauffeur. Even though my mom had a ride home, I was still boiling mad at my brother's unwillingness to help.

When I returned to the room, my mom's eyes were open. Before I could stop myself, I blurted, "I can't believe Jun-chan didn't come today. Can't get up in the morning? Too much traffic? Give me a fucking break."

"It was your fault," she snapped.

"Why was it my fault?" I shouted.

"You were supposed to call him and give him a heads-up. He didn't come because you never called him!"

I was quite familiar with that stern tone of voice. She used it to say unkind things when her emotions got the best of her. It reminded me of all the times I'd said mean things to David and Peter when my emotions were out of control.

"That's ridiculous. He's an adult! He's not here because he's so selfish. I despise him!"

She raised herself up on one elbow. "Don't you dare say such a thing," she scolded with a frown. Then after a pause, she added in a gentler tone, "I want you kids to get along."

But Hiro-chan, Jun-chan, and I had grown up totally separate from each other. How could my mother not see how hopelessly estranged we were?

A nurse hurried in with a dinner tray and a cup of tea. "Make sure you record how much liquid she takes," she said to me, handing me a clipboard. "Here's the sheet to fill out the time and the amount. She needs to drink plenty of fluids for this IV to work properly."

My mom had a hard time feeding herself with both her arms taped. She bent her right arm to hold the chopsticks while attempting to grab a piece of fish, but it kept sliding off. The dinner didn't look terribly appetizing, either—grilled red snapper, pickled cucumbers and carrots, shredded cabbage, slices of mushy tomato with rice, and skimpy miso soup with a lone piece of seaweed floating near the top. I felt sorry for her and tried to help her eat, but she said things like, "Don't give me that," "I don't like carrots," and "Peel off that skin."

I sighed. She was even more finicky than David had been in kindergarten.

"Enough," she said, pushing the tray away. "No more."

"Mom, you haven't eaten anything since this morning. And you've got to eat more vegetables too."

As she reluctantly took a bite of fish from the chopsticks I held, I started to unravel. She looked so passive, frail, and vulnerable, a stark contrast to the vibrant, charismatic woman I'd known. My mind flashed back to the time I visited my dad at the nursing home and tried to feed him. He had trouble swallowing, and the food I managed to put into his mouth spilled out over and over again. I burst into tears, not knowing how to help him.

I didn't want my mom to get upset seeing me cry, so I stared at the tiny TV screen as if I was absorbed in the program.

Dr. Nakamura entered the room and saw me wipe away my tears. He stared at me for a moment, then asked in a cheerful voice, "How are things?"

"Okay, I guess," I answered with a forced smile. "I'd better leave soon, or we'll get into a fight."

"Please, help her gently," he said with a charming smile. Then he bowed and said in English, "See you . . ."

I helped him finish, "See you again?"

"Yes, see you again," he repeated in English.

In truth, I didn't want to see him again, no matter how attractive he was, because that would mean my mom would be back here sometime in the future.

After he left, I helped her to the bathroom. I recorded the amount of liquid she'd taken and got her more tea from the nurses' station. I then gathered my stuff, put on my coat, and said, "Get some good rest, Mom. I'll see you tomorrow."

I took the elevator down to the lobby and stepped outside. Walking to the train station in the dark, I felt a sense of relief, layered with inexplicable sorrow. I was glad things hadn't been worse for her. But at the same time, I couldn't help feeling my mother's absence so much more intensely. I longed for the kind of mother I could depend on for solace when I'd actually needed a break from being a mother. Why had I thought this time would be any different? I didn't come back here to mother my own mother. *I don't even know how to mother myself, for God's sake.*

As I stood alone on the unusually empty train platform, a gust of cold wind struck me. I turned up my coat collar and secured the silk scarf around my neck. A fluorescent light nearby flickered over a vending machine, and I considered buying myself some hot corn soup to warm up, but I was too distraught. Back in January when I had returned for my dad's funeral, I had a glimpse of how disconnected and estranged we all were as a family, but we still managed to come together for the occasion. That time, I'd only been here for five days; I'd gone home relatively unscathed. But not on this trip.

After ten days, I was tired of interacting with my mom. I still hadn't seen Hiro-chan except briefly the night before. He hadn't participated in our dad's death anniversary ceremony either. I knew he had his own struggles with mental health, but the last time I saw him during our dad's funeral in January, he seemed happy to see me. I wondered if he was intentionally avoiding me this time. I also hadn't seen my niece and her family yet, even though they, including our mother, lived in the same apartment building just a few meters from each other. They avoided interacting at all costs, and no one seemed happy. Dad was gone, and the family was damaged way beyond repair. We were too far gone. It was too late.

What about my family in Seattle? Was it too late for us as well?

On a cold, crisp day in early December, I went to the Chinese herb pharmacy in Tokyo that my friend Yukiko had recommended. Yukiko had been suffering severe hot flashes, but the symptom had improved significantly with customized concoctions of Chinese herbs prescribed at the pharmacy. She'd spent 1,000 yen ($10.00 USD) a day during the peak of her symptoms but was now spending about 400 yen ($4.00 USD) a day. There was no way I'd spend that much, but she still urged me to go and talk with the chief herbalist since the consultation was free.

The pharmacy was small but well-lit, clean, and organized. Most of the products were displayed neatly, stacked on the walls behind the front counter. Some herbs were inside large, clear glass jars, and others were prepackaged in rectangular boxes covered with Chinese characters.

I sat at the consultation table across from the chief herbalist, who looked dignified and confident in her white gown. She was in her early sixties, tall, thin, and full of vitality. Her mannerisms communicated a devout faith in the medicine she sold. Her herbalist-in-training daughter stood behind her. I answered a series of questions regarding my medical history and current symptoms, diet, and sleep patterns. I then described my chronic pain, anxiety, and irritability.

The herbalist took my pulse and then asked to see my tongue. She and her daughter both gazed at it, and the chief said, "Oh, yeah, it's showing," and her daughter said, "Yeah, it sure is."

What was showing? I was dying to ask what they meant. What if they'd seen a sign that I was losing my mind? *Better to keep quiet.*

The chief herbalist looked at me intently. "Can you sleep?"

"Yes, my sleep is okay. I'm taking Sedaplex, an herbal sleep aid." Actually, I was taking Lunesta, but I didn't want to reveal that because herbalists are typically anti-pharmaceuticals, and she would have urged me to stop taking it right away. I wasn't ready for that.

Her daughter searched the internet for information on Sedaplex. "Oh no, a bunch of English I don't understand."

"You are highly sensitive with a very delicate nervous system," the chief herbalist said. "So, during menopause, your preexisting conditions, like irritability, were exacerbated."

"How long will it last?" I asked.

She steepled her long fingers. "It can span over five years before and five years after menopause. But once you get through this period, your life will improve."

This shattering revelation almost knocked me to the floor. "You mean ten years?"

She nodded. It meant I still had several years to go.

At the end of the intake session I mentioned Yukiko's customized Chinese herbs. The chief said, "I can make it a little cheaper for you. Three hundred yen ($3.00 USD) a day. Would that work?"

But with the additional supplements, I ended up paying about $500 for a three-month supply. It was more than I'd been willing to spend initially, but Yukiko had highly recommended her. Plus, the herbalist's piercing looks and assertive behavior made her doubly convincing—and I was desperate.

During the last week of my "convalescence" trip, my American friend Helen came to visit from Seattle, and we went sightseeing for a week. It was a welcome respite from my Japanese family and helped me regain my sanity. We had a great time visiting many places in Tokyo, Kyoto, and Hakone. In a Kyoto temple, we saw the fall foliage lit up at night, and the place transformed into a dream world of massive red, orange, and yellow leaves that was absolutely breathtaking. I felt proud to be Japanese.

But that sense of pride evaporated the day before flying back to Seattle when Helen and I took a train to do some last-minute souvenir shopping. It was late morning and passengers were sparse. I gestured to Helen to sit down, and I stood in front of her, holding onto a strap. We'd already talked so much throughout our trip, but there was still more to discuss. I yakked continuously while Helen listened. A guy in his twenties sat on Helen's left, wearing a mask, and a middle-aged guy sat on her right, but I didn't pay any attention to them. Nor did I realize I was the only person on the train who was talking.

Several minutes into my chatter, the younger guy suddenly pulled down his mask and yelled at me, "Damareyo! Uruseendayo!" ("Shut the fuck up! You are so goddamn noisy!")

I was startled. "I'm sorry. It's been so long since I've been in this country. I've forgotten the customs."

"That's no excuse," he said with a piercing glare.

I was dumbfounded and gave Helen an awkward grin.

"What are you smiling about?" he said angrily. "Are you mocking me?"

I kept my face blank and avoided eye contact with him. He might be a *chinpira*, a low-ranking gangster. He certainly behaved like one. I was horrified but, at the same time, angry. I felt like kicking him and calling him an asshole. But I kept my temper in check, which was wise because if he was indeed a *chinpira*, he might have pulled out a pocketknife and stabbed me.

I thought that was the end of it, but then the older gentleman turned to me and said, "He's right, you know. I kept waiting to see when you would shut up, and you never did." His eyes were narrowed, and his jaw was tense. But I refused to offer any more obsequious apologies.

"Oh my God," said Helen after we got off the train. "Those guys were so aggressive."

I kept walking until we were at a safe distance away before telling her what the thuggish guy had said to me.

Helen was outraged. "Is it Japanese etiquette to stay silent on trains? Certainly not in the United States. Even so, his response was totally out of line. So ironic that he ended up being way more disruptive than you were."

Yes, I had violated the tacit Japanese etiquette to be discreet and refrain from talking on trains, and that was shameful. But I also noticed something else: This was my third time being yelled at by an angry male that year (first by Jun-chan, then Peter, and now this thug). It made me wonder if my blabbermouth provoked males to explode in anger.

This rail rage incident, however, was the most jarring of the times, and it left me with mild PTSD for months. Thus, the trip ended on a sour note and only deepened my despondency.

Biscuit

December 15, 2015 to January 24, 2016

As soon as I walked through my front door after the long flight from Japan, I collapsed into bed. In a stupor, I anxiously waited for David to return from school, with fingers crossed for good news.

I'd planned the extended trip to Japan to buy myself enough time to regain the stamina I needed to deal with issues at home in Seattle. Whether or not I was ready to face reality, I still looked forward to reuniting with my family. I chose to return on "Judgment Day" for high school seniors nationwide, the day when they'd hear about their early college application results. I wanted to be there for David in case he needed my moral support. But I also hoped it would be a time to celebrate. I'd made my pilgrimage to several school shrines while in Japan and had even paid extra to partake in a special Shinto *Oharai* purification ceremony at Yushima Tenmangu near the University of Tokyo. This was Tokyo's most famous shrine of scholars, a power spot believed to bring academic success.

Unfortunately, I had come home utterly exhausted and miserable. I felt the full weight of the Chinese herbalist's pronouncement that menopause had been exacerbating my physical and emotional symptoms and that it would take close to ten years to get out of the menopausal woods.

Aside from my usual chronic aches and pains, I'd been triple-whammied by jet lag, a nasty cold, and a throbbing pain in my gums from a lingual nerve injury I'd inadvertently inflicted on myself while in Japan.

While waiting for David, I recalled several of the difficult events on my trip and realized I felt worse now than when I'd left. Being around my Japanese family was like stepping on hidden emotional land mines and reopening old wounds. My age-old grudge resurfaced from feeling emotionally abandoned by my family, and I felt like a victim all over again. I found myself reacting from the place of the wounded child with limited and ineffectual coping skills. The family therapist had pointed this out the previous year, but I'd ignored it. I now wished I'd taken her words seriously and been more proactive to prevent further damage to my family.

While all these thoughts swirled in my head, David came home crying. He entered my bedroom looking totally dejected, his fists clenched. I braced myself for the heartbreaking news and gave him a warm hug as he sat down next to me. My body tightened, heart pounding, and I felt the cold sensation of blood draining from my head, but I pretended to be unfazed.

"I got deferred from Yale," he said in a barely audible voice. "What's really upsetting is that everyone else in my class who applied early action to Yale got accepted."

"How many students applied?" My hands shook, but fortunately, David couldn't see them in the dark room.

"Six, including me," he said, wiping his tears.

I flashed back to the day I had participated in the *Oharai* ceremony at *Yushima Tenmangu*. I don't remember exactly how much

I paid, but it was more than the suggested amount of 5,000 yen (approximately $50 USD). I might even have paid double, thinking the more I spent, the better the outcome would be. It wasn't the time to be a cheapskate. Before the ceremony the priest had checked each participant's request and looked at me, puzzled.

"Only one school? Are you sure?" he asked.

"Yes," I said.

One of the limitations of the "restrictive early action" applications to four of the most prestigious colleges (Harvard, Yale, Princeton, and Stanford) was that a student was only allowed to apply for early action to one of them. I knew little about Yale, and it wasn't even close to my top choice for David, but it was unequivocally his. The ceremony at the shrine in Japan was solemn and so deeply moving that I wept throughout, though the physical and emotional exhaustion from both sleep deprivation and being around my mom likely contributed to my emotional imbalance. But now reality set in. I could have paid more. I should have. I knew how high the stakes were.

But then I looked at David, bright-eyed. "That's *so* not the end of the world. It was a big-reach school, and they didn't flat-out reject you. You still have a chance." I was, however, skeptical they'd accept any more students from his high school. "You'll be fine. Just get busy applying to other schools, okay?" I pretended to be chipper, but underneath I was coming apart. I wanted this nightmarish college admission process to be over as soon as possible. Three more agonizing months of cliff-hangers felt like an eternity.

I changed the subject. "Oh hey, I brought you what you asked for. Come take a look."

His face lit up.

As we walked downstairs to my still-unopened suitcase, I said, "I don't get the hype—they look like overpriced ordinary shirts with a creepy logo. But talk about playing hard to get. I called several Comme des Garçons PLAY stores, but either things were sold out or they wouldn't set merchandise aside. So I took a chance and showed up at a store in Shibuya to see what was available." I fished out two long-sleeve cotton shirts, one white and one blue-striped, each boasting a red heart applique logo with cat eyes.

David looked happy to have these highly coveted shirts. He immediately tried them on and said, "Thanks, Mom. These are great."

It was just what he needed to lift his spirits. All the hassle I'd undergone the day before my departure to make it to the store—hustling through crowded rush-hour trains for two hours all the way to Shibuya (famous for its iconic crosswalk, the world's busiest)—had been worth it.

Within days, I learned from David that all his classmates and friends of Asian descent had been either rejected or deferred from other colleges during this early round—even Connor, an outstanding model student with perfect ACT scores, who was the class president, a team captain in many sports, and an Eagle Scout.

I was shocked but shouldn't have been, given the warning from the director of college counseling services during the information session in early fall. Pointing to a 5 percent acceptance rate, he'd said, "After the spots are taken by their institutional priority students, like elite athletes, legacies, underrepresented minorities, students who would be the first in their families to attend college, and those with *wow* factors, the acceptance rate for the rest of the applicants without such hooks drops down to 1 percent."

One thing that the director had not mentioned, but that Peter and I had read about, was the use of racial quotas for Asian students in highly selective schools (a 20 percent cap on Asian and Asian American students), just as had been applied to Jewish-American students in the 1920s. Their selection process was not only highly political and rigged but also discriminatory. I had also read about the unsavory practice of aggressively recruiting students and then rejecting them in order to artificially drive down schools' acceptance rates so that they appeared even more selective. It all seemed like a game.

Thus began my anti-Yale psychosis, a near-pathological emotional preoccupation and obsession with the school that had rejected my son. One day when I was feeling especially wrathful, I reached out to my American "brother" Ricky, who jokingly suggested that I make a Yale pennant out of paper and set it on fire. I did, not just once, but three times. I didn't stop there. I took one out to our stone patio, stomped all over it, and then jumped up and down on it.

"Aaaahhh!" Peter said, one day covering his ears. "All you do is rant about Yale. I don't want to hear about this anymore." He went to the other room. He was also concerned that I was depleting my limited emotional energy by taking David's rejection too personally. I knew I was driving him nuts but didn't care. I was obsessed.

While David bounced back quickly from the setback and shifted his focus to other schools, my struggle with rejection dejection was gathering momentum. I must have subconsciously internalized his initial pain as if it were mine. My own ancient pains came back to haunt me, as each time the image of David coming home sobbing flashed through my mind, I was retraumatized. It evoked something visceral in me—how chagrined I'd felt when I hadn't even bothered applying to Futaba or Shirayuri Gakuen, the middle schools of my dreams, because I thought they'd been way out of reach for me. I was envious of classmates who'd been accepted to those girls' schools and got to wear the adorable sailor uniforms. I tested into a decent girls' school but still felt like a failure, having to go through the daily humiliating experience in the competitive primary school environment where students' statuses were determined by which prestigious middle schools had accepted them. But my parents had no idea how hard I took it because I never told them.

This early action school experience only amplified my feelings of worthlessness, instilling at the same time a deep sense of inadequacy and inferiority—lifelong wounds I had yet to overcome. How I wished I'd had parents who could have helped me outgrow my childish and unhealthy all-or-nothing mindset.

My stubborn grudge against Yale inspired me to write a three-page letter to William Deresiewicz, the author of *Excellent Sheep*, in which he illuminated the problems with elite college admissions. I shared my traumatic experience of credential-oriented schooling in Japan and expressed my outrage over American elitism and the rigged college admissions system in the United States. I was dismayed to find myself steeped in the same abominable mentality I thought I'd long moved away from. Writing to him was amazingly cathartic, and I was pleasantly surprised to receive a thoughtful and supportive response.

There were many pressing issues to worry about in my life: my mother's deteriorating health, my Japanese family's devastating estrangement, David's relationship with Ana, and the growing rift in my marriage. But I set these aside, convincing myself that my vehement animosity against Yale was the most urgent.

I was creating my own living hell. My daily calls to check on my mom only depressed me more because she was so despondent and fatalistic. When David and Ana were quiet behind his closed bedroom door, I'd frequently knock and say, "Hey guys, make sure you practice safe sex," and worry that she might get pregnant. Then it wouldn't be a matter of which college might accept him, as his entire future would be in jeopardy.

I had few coping skills and could only think in absolutes, and now my out-of-control worries took on a life of their own. Ever since the Ana fiasco had begun in late August, I'd started losing my appetite. Over the following four months, consumed by daily stress and anxiety over matters beyond my control, I lost ten pounds. I was living on Chobani yogurt and ready-to-eat hard-boiled eggs (the most fantastic innovation since sliced bread). By the end of the year, with my five-foot frame, I weighed only ninety-three pounds—the skinniest I'd been since I was a teenager. Although I liked how loosely my clothes fit, I felt weak and listless.

One morning in late December, with no regard for how Peter might feel, I blurted, "I just can't take all this stress anymore. I need to get away." I was being just like my mom, who'd make the same careless remarks whenever she felt desperate or exasperated—though I couldn't see it at the time.

"You just came back," he grumbled, then stared at my disheveled appearance and shook his head. "Going away won't solve your problems. You need to do something constructive."

I ignored his advice and started daydreaming about taking a real vacation.

That afternoon, while Peter and David were out at Home Depot, I was struck by powerful feelings of loneliness and isolation. I recognized then that they were of my own doing. I valued my need for solitude over participating in family activities and then felt bad for being excluded. A sense of helplessness swept over me. How much longer could I go on like this? I felt just as I had when I was a child, left alone to deal with inexplicable sadness and loneliness—trapped, with no place to hide or escape to.

When I saw Biscuit lying at the bottom of staircase as she often did, I went over to hug her and buried my face in her fur, soft as cotton. I inhaled deeply and then curled up next to her and sniffed her fur, her paw, her ear. I found her subtle, earthy scent—an odd combination of slightly burned popcorn, roasted chestnuts, and Asiago cheese—so calming and comforting. Focusing my attention on Biscuit helped me stay grounded in the moment. I felt solace in her affection and unconditional love, just as I had with her predecessors.

Unlike Amber, who was very independent and aloof, Biscuit was like a goofy, huggable polar bear. She always greeted us with such enthusiasm, as if she'd never had a bad day in her life. A highly sensitive and empathic soul, she was always tuned in to our emotions. Being a pacifist who didn't like conflict, she'd leave the room whenever a heated argument broke out. She brought smiles to our faces with her whimsical behavior, like when her long, fluffy tail would go *whack, whack, whack* every time we approached to pet her.

When Peter and David came home, I was still on the floor with Biscuit.

David knelt next to me and jostled my shoulder. "Mom, are you okay?"

I looked up. Something in my expression must have given me away because Peter said, "You're not doing well. You need to see a psychiatrist. A real psychiatrist, not a talk therapist."

"No, I'll be fine," I replied, but I didn't put up much fuss. I knew he was right.

Within a few days, through internal arrangements, he put me in touch with a reputable psychiatrist. Although she wasn't accepting new patients, upon Peter's urgent request she agreed to take me.

Three weeks later, I was in her office, stepping on a scale. I'd gained two pounds, with the scale hovering around ninety-five. Small progress, but progress. Her office was remarkably cluttered and disorganized, with papers and books stacked on her desk and scattered on the floor. But such chaos was not reflected in her personality. In her mid-sixties with chin-length, wavy gray hair, she was attentive and had a warm presence that put me at ease.

At the end of the intake session, she diagnosed me with generalized anxiety disorder and told me I needed to take an antidepressant. I told her I'd taken Venlafaxine for several years but had abruptly quit nine months ago.

Her eyebrows rose. "Cold turkey? Your doctor allowed that?"

I hung my head. "I didn't consult my doctor. I thought I was better."

"You shouldn't have stopped," she said. Because of my childhood trauma from emotional neglect, she explained, I was still PTSD-ish, and my vulnerability to stress and anxiety would likely be with me forever.

"Besides," she added, "compared to other antidepressants, Venlafaxine is one of the hardest ones to wean off and causes severe and prolonged withdrawal symptoms. It can be debilitating even when tapered off slowly."

No wonder I'd been so out of sorts.

While she was writing out a new prescription, I aired my grievances about the college application process and the whole Yale thing. I also mentioned there was a school concert that night.

"David will be playing violin, but I don't want to go because I don't want to see the parents whose kids were accepted to Yale." I furrowed my brow like a petulant child.

She slid her glasses down her nose and looked at me. "That's silly. You should go if your son is playing."

She was right. But that was how the wounded child inside me reacted, no matter how ridiculous it was. I snuck into the concert hall and sat in the back to watch him perform. He exuded confidence, and I was glad I had come. Still, as soon as the concert was over, I hurried out.

One evening in late January, a dozen of David's classmates showed up at our front door, saying they'd come for an intervention. Some of them were his close friends, while others were a random assortment of classmates who'd apparently come along for the ride. I let them into the living room, where they waited for him to come home.

When David arrived and saw them all there, his jaw dropped with a WTF expression. Off they went to his man cave downstairs, where they stayed for a few hours. I was concerned but kept my distance.

When they left, I braced myself for drama, but David was in a good mood.

"It was more of a practical joke," he said, "but they tried to persuade me to break up with Ana. They don't think she's good for me." He seemed both amused and touched by the well-meaning gesture. He also said he realized just how much social life he'd been missing by ditching his friends first for Liz and then for Ana.

This time I made an effort to stay out of his business to avoid repeating the mistake I'd made by meddling in his relationship with Liz. When he eventually broke up with Ana about two months later, I asked if it had something to do with that intervention.

"Well, maybe," he said. "But when she called me about forty times while I was on a bro camping trip, I couldn't take it anymore."

It was a relief to know he had good friends and could judge a bad romance for himself without needing me to intervene.

On the last Friday in January, I took Biscuit for her regular checkup and acupuncture. The holistic vet she saw wasn't cheap, but after treating Biscuit's arthritis and skin problems with acupuncture and Chinese herbs for several months, I'd seen some progress.

But the next morning Biscuit struggled to get up on her hind legs. I shouted for Peter. "Something's wrong with Biscuit! She can't get up!" Panic washed over me as we carried her to the car and raced her to an emergency veterinary clinic.

This was my third time taking a dying dog to an emergency room. It was a gut-wrenching experience. I started to cry and put my head on Peter's shoulder while waiting for the vet to give us an update. Life seemed so unfair and cruel. My mind raced with regrets. I kept wondering why the holistic vet hadn't caught this the day before. Had the acupuncture caused this? Or maybe it had been the Chinese herbs. Was the medicated shampoo I used on her too toxic? Maybe I hadn't taken her on enough walks. I wondered if it was true that empathic dogs absorb negativity in the household and get sick.

When the vet finally came out, he said, "Seems like she had a stroke. I observed her, and she kept turning in one direction when she tried to get up. We can do a CT scan to determine the cause."

"Will she get better?" My voice quivered.

He shook his head. "No, probably not."

"What will we do with the information then?" I asked.

"Some people like to find out."

"Then, no," I said. "That would be pointless. We have to let her go."

After a moment of silence, Peter said, "Could you keep her here for a while—a day maybe—so we can prepare ourselves?"

"Of course," the vet said.

I cried all the way home and off and on for the rest of that day. Peter teared up, too, but he was more restrained. I was so upset with the holistic vet that I threw away the expensive Chinese herbs. Wrenching grief shook me to my already fragile core. Another devastating blow.

When Shelly, my sheltie companion of eleven years, had suddenly collapsed in our Minnesota apartment, Peter and I had also rushed her to the vet. While the veterinarian examined her, she slipped into unconsciousness, urinating on the table before her body went limp. We knew this was a bad sign. The vet carried her to the back room to revive her. Within a few minutes, he returned with the bad news and asked if we wanted to say goodbye. Crying and distraught, we said no. The vet understood. We wanted to remember her as the happy, vibrant dog she'd been, not a lifeless body. Twelve years later, Nikki, our golden retriever, passed away from sarcoma. Experiencing these deaths with Peter had brought us even closer together. With Biscuit, it would be our first experience of having to euthanize a dog.

That night, Peter and I lay in bed, unable to fall asleep.

"I don't think I can bring myself to put Biscuit down tomorrow," I said. "It'll be too traumatic for me."

"You don't have to go," he said. "I'll go with David."

"Thank you for staying so strong." I hugged him and kissed him on the cheek. "I love you."

It surprised me to hear those words come out of my mouth. I rarely told him I loved him. Maybe it had something to do with my cultural inhibition or my upbringing: overt verbal expressions of love and affection were not something I'd grown up with. But maybe at a deeper level, I was also afraid of his response. A decade earlier, when he'd stopped telling me he loved me, I had partially assumed he was merely responding in kind, not because of his lack of love for me. Or so I wanted to believe. Maybe I was in denial, and, in fact, he'd given up on us after feeling rejected and hurt by me too many times.

Now, I waited for him to respond. When he didn't say anything, I leaned over and looked at him.

After a moment of silence, he said, "I'm working on it."

"What?" I sat up. "Don't you love me anymore? What would I do without you?" My voice shook. Was our marriage dying too? I felt raw and more vulnerable than ever before, as if the many wounds of my childhood had been ripped wide open.

But I was so grief-stricken over Biscuit that I couldn't absorb any more sadness. Something shifted inside me—maybe it was my survival instinct kicking in. I knew I couldn't afford to collapse into despair. I had to get through this somehow. So instead of sinking into a black hole, I said to myself, *I can only handle one sadness at a time. This will have to wait until I'm ready.* All night I repeated in my head, *One thing at a time. One thing at a time*, like a mantra to lull myself to sleep.

But at the same time, something was awakening in me. Maybe it was the trips home to see my family and the reckoning I'd done in their aftermath, but this round of crises awoke a sleeping giant, my inner strength. This blow would have flattened the fragile self I'd been a year earlier.

Looking back, I can see now that during the twenty years of our marriage and my struggles with motherhood, I'd become too dependent on Peter, not just financially but also emotionally, and I had steadily lost my sense of self. Just like my mom, who was trapped in learned helplessness.

When we'd met at Stanford, I was thriving in that intellectually stimulating environment. But I was no longer the happy and confident person he'd married, and over time, he'd come to see that. I couldn't blame him for struggling to stay with me. I'd pulled a bait and switch on him.

I still had a ways to go to rebuild my self-confidence, but my determination to get through that heartrending period was a sure sign that I had grown stronger. I was shifting my rusty gears to revive myself and move in the right direction so that I could take charge of my life again.

The next evening, Peter and David went back to the clinic to say goodbye to Biscuit. An hour later they returned, shoulders slumped, on the verge of tears. Peter told me that when Biscuit had been rolled into the exam room on a cart, as soon as she saw them, she raised her head and wagged her tail—*whack, whack, whack*—against the cart. He didn't think he could manage staying with Biscuit when she received the injection, so when the vet assistant rolled Biscuit back out, he and David returned to the lobby. But a moment later, David dashed into the staff-only part of the clinic where Biscuit was about to be put down. David stayed with her until she took her last breath, and then met up with Peter in the lobby. They hugged and walked quietly to the car. They hardly spoke on the way home. It said a lot about David's strength, courage, and compassion. I couldn't be prouder of who he'd become.

"She looked comfortable, Mom, and . . . and went very peacefully in my arms," he said, choking back tears.

"You are so strong and brave. Thank you for being there for her," I said, crying and squeezing him. All three of us huddled up in a group hug and bawled together.

Biscuit died two months shy of her eighth birthday, the same age our golden retriever, Nikki, had been at her death in 2008. The passings of these beloved companions were excruciating to me, but I wished something good would come from the immense sorrow. With Biscuit's death, perhaps because my life seemed to be closing in on me, that sentiment became even more pronounced this time. And I hoped our shared grief would bring our family closer together again.

Holland America

October 15, 2016

It was the beginning of another lazy weekend when I felt like cuddling up to Peter and staying in bed past 9:00 a.m. Except that when I turned over to reach for him, he wasn't there. I didn't even smell coffee brewing, which usually marked the start of our weekend together. I looked at my alarm clock: 7:30 a.m. Why was he up so early? He always slept in on weekends. Normally, I would have gone back to sleep, but I was curious to see what he was up to. I got out of bed, rubbed my sleepy eyes, and went downstairs. He sat in the kitchen, staring at the table.

"What are you doing down here?" I asked.

He looked at me, his salt-and-pepper hair sticking up in cowlicks, dark circles under his eyes, his expression tormented. "I have something important to tell you," he said. He got up, pulled out two kitchen chairs, and arranged them facing each other. "Take a seat."

Heart pounding, jaw tightening with growing apprehension, I sat down, holding my breath.

He looked deep into my eyes and said, "I'm moving out."

"What?" I grabbed the edges of the chair, afraid I might fall.

"I've been unhappy for a long time," he said with sadness in his eyes. "It was a mistake for us to get married. We didn't even know each other that well. We're so different. We have different interests, even different senses of humor. David's out of the house now. He's stable and off to a good start at Columbia. This hasn't been an easy decision, but I need to do it. For myself."

At first, I was so stunned I couldn't say a word. Blood rushed from my head down to my feet. I held back my tears. "Please give me a chance. Let's start over."

We talked for about an hour—or rather, I listened as he calmly explained his issues with our relationship and why he decided he had to leave. And then he walked out.

I remained at the kitchen table, lost in thought for a long time. *What just happened?* I stared blankly out the window at a hummingbird landing on the feeder. My mind flashed back to the summer I had turned sixteen, the first time I'd seen a hummingbird outside the kitchen window of my host family's home in California. Ever since Joanne introduced it to me as her favorite bird, it had been mine too.

Hummingbirds were a symbolic reminder of Joanne's loving presence and her happy home. I'd created a backyard hummingbird garden myself, filled with hummer-friendly plants. Although I'd come to take hummers for granted since they stuck around all year in Seattle, they never ceased to remind me of Joanne. I thought of her often in passing, but today I missed her so much more. I wished I could talk with her. She had died of cancer when David was only sixteen months old, but I suddenly realized that even after eighteen years, I still hadn't allowed myself to grieve her.

Joanne was a highly spiritual person. When she kept appearing in my dreams, still alive and vibrant, I somehow came to believe that she would always be around me in spirit. Now, looking back, it was a form of denial and dissociation that had helped me survive the dark period. I was in the throes of postpartum depression, and I emotionally shut down to avoid descending further into an abyss, dealing with the enormity of losing her. I'd been unaware this same emotional distancing and numbing had become so habitual that it destroyed our marriage.

My throat tightened as I remembered the summer when I'd pledged to choose happiness and to create a happy, loving family just like hers. *How could I have let all this happen?*

Amber came over to check on me and then jumped onto my lap. My eyes welled as I buried my face in her soft, curly fur. A dozen years earlier, about a month before Peter had almost left, I'd brought this teddy bear look-alike home from a nearby pet store. Back then, I was just as unhappy (or perhaps even unhappier) as he was, so Amber was truly a godsend. I told Peter I *had* to rescue her because nobody wanted her and bragged that I got a real bargain—one-tenth the cost my mother paid for her own toy poodle in Japan, where this breed was the latest canine trend. *Too good to pass up*, I'd told myself. *A sign from heaven.*

"Return her," Peter said sternly. "We already have Nikki." Nikki was four years old at the time.

"No!" I snapped like a cranky, obstinate child. "You can't tell me what to do. I'm an adult. I get to do what I want." Amber represented an overdue solace I felt I needed, a step in the direction toward self-care. A shot in the dark for someone who had no idea what it meant to take care of herself.

Grudgingly, he agreed to let me keep her. I was surprised by how quickly and easily he caved in. Perhaps it was a sign he'd already given up on us and was ready to file for divorce. It was less than a month later that he had his grand mal seizure, and I found out he had consulted a divorce lawyer. *What's the point of putting up a fuss over yet another dog when I'm about to walk out the door?* he must have thought. Learning about the lawyer was shocking and then devastating—even more so than his developing epilepsy. I felt betrayed—a wound from which I hadn't fully recovered. But in retrospect, the apparent misfortune of his sudden illness had kept our marriage going for twelve more years. I thought we'd persevered and had overcome our difficulties, but he might have simply chickened out after sensing his own mortality.

I went upstairs and checked his drawers and closet. They were all empty. Like the air, I'd taken his steady presence for granted. Now that he was gone, I felt his absence intensely. Too shell-shocked and dismayed to cry, I stumbled around the house, searching for something to occupy my mind. I cleaned out my closet, a chore I'd been putting off for years. I had too many clothes. There were even scarves with the price tags still attached. I couldn't remember when or where I'd bought them. It was a painful reminder of how unfulfilled I'd been and how much money I'd wasted trying to fill the deep void inside me.

And where had I learned that ineffective coping strategy? I flashed back to an evening at Mom's apartment when she'd searched drawer after drawer to find something useful for me. She pulled out several pairs of Christian Dior underwear with the price tags still attached. "You can use these, can't you?"

No matter how much I despised her overspending habit, no matter how hard I tried not to be like her, it had been a losing battle. I had become exactly like her. But at the same time, I now understood the sadness and emptiness she'd felt deep inside her that nothing or no one could ever fill.

I managed to get through the day without crying—mainly by

preoccupying myself with organizing my closet. But bedtime was another story. As soon as I lay down, my mind raced. We might be heading for divorce and this time for real.

In the nine months since Biscuit's death, I'd thought we'd made progress, learning to communicate and understand each other and get along better, but Peter had already built an emotional fortress around his heart. He'd lost hope in our marriage, he said, and was moving to an apartment near his office in downtown Seattle.

I'd been lying in bed for forty-five minutes with no sign of the sleep aid I'd taken kicking in. I felt his side of the bed, now empty. With each shallow breath, every muscle grew increasingly tense. The pitch-black darkness created by the blackout curtains now felt dense, almost suffocating. Silence loomed large and overwhelming, just like it had when I was a child after the housekeeper had left for the day and I was alone in the house.

Whenever my nervous system got revved up like this, even doubling the Lunesta dose wouldn't help me sleep. I got out of bed and shuffled downstairs to the medicine cabinet section of the pantry, desperate for more sedatives. Toward the back, behind the Aleve, progesterone, and melatonin, I found the Xanax my doctor had prescribed a few years before for my fear of flying. I cut one in half and swallowed it dry. I then found an old bottle of hydrocodone, expired for seven years. I hesitated. Should I take half? A whole? I'd never downed a cocktail of drugs before but decided to take one of those too.

I went back to bed, but after thirty minutes my mind was still racing. How would I go on? I'd tried my hardest to raise David, and he was now happy and thriving at Columbia. It was a huge relief to see that despite my haphazard approach to parenting, I had somehow managed to break the cycle of emotional neglect for him, and he had come out unscathed. In a recent phone call I was moved to tears when he told me his core values to live by were kindness, humility, gratitude, self-reliance, and boldness.

Yes, I did the best I could, so no regrets, I kept telling myself. But despite my efforts to rationalize, my thoughts careened in familiar catastrophic patterns. *David's gone now, and my job as a mother is done. Peter's gone, too, so there's no reason for me to be here anymore.*

For a moment, I wished I could disappear and go somewhere for a reprieve, but there was no way I'd go back to Japan this time.

Suddenly, a dark thought crossed my mind. *What if I just end it?*

Nearly all day I'd controlled my impulse to call Peter. I didn't want to seem needy and was also afraid of his indifference. But still wide awake at 11:30 p.m. and overcome by a fear of the unknown and my suicidal thoughts, I decided to call him. The call went directly to voicemail. At first, I didn't know what to say, only that it needed to be dramatic enough to catch his attention so he wouldn't ignore me. I left a shaky voice message.

"I'm feeling suicidal and scared. Should I call 911?" And then I hung up.

About fifteen minutes later, the phone rang. The caller ID registered "Holland America." *Who the hell is Holland America? What a ridiculous name. And how rude to call this late.* Still, for some reason, I picked up the phone.

"Are you okay?" the male caller asked timidly.

"What?" I had no idea who this was.

"You left a message. It sounded very serious."

Oh. My. God. "I'm so sorry, I must have misdialed. The message was meant for my husband. He just moved out this morning and I've been so upset."

There was a moment of silence. "Are you gonna be okay though?"

"Yeah, I'll be fine. Thanks for your concern. It's very kind of you to check on me. I'll manage. Thank you." Hanging up the phone, I flushed with embarrassment.

A few minutes later, the phone rang again. This time the caller ID read "Seattle Police Department." *Oh my gosh. What have I done?* One wrong number and now the police were involved.

I picked up the phone. Before I could say a word a woman said, "Hello, ma'am? A gentleman just called and asked if we could check on you. He was very concerned. Are you okay?"

I explained the situation, including the misdial, and assured her I was fine.

"Would you like to talk with some officers?" she asked. "I can dispatch them to your house if you'd like."

I contemplated it for a moment. *There's nothing wrong with accepting help.* "Okay, sure," I said. "That would be nice."

Half an hour later, two policemen, clean-shaven with military haircuts, showed up at my front door. They introduced themselves, but I immediately forgot their names, so in my mind they were Officer 1 and Officer 2. Officer 1 was white, blond, of medium stature, and in his mid-to-late thirties. Officer 2 was African American, slightly taller and thinner, and in his twenties. Both had calm, reassuring demeanors with warm smiles. I was in my sloppy pajamas and slippers, my hair disheveled. I sat down on the bottom stair, holding Amber while they remained standing in the entryway. The meds I'd taken earlier had finally kicked in, and I felt relaxed and uninhibited.

"Are you still in danger of harming yourself?" Officer 1 asked.

"Hell, no," I said, surprised that the word "hell" had come out.

"Have you been drinking, ma'am?" asked Officer 2.

"Oh no, I don't drink. Why? Do I seem drunk?"

Officer 1 shrugged and gave a palms-up "I dunno" gesture.

"I took a few sedatives, but that's all." I waved a hand, trying to downplay it. "My mention of suicide was just a passing impulsive thought."

I shared a brief version of what had happened in my life. Then I explained how a guy named Holland America had gotten involved, all because I'd misdialed my husband's number.

"How long have you two been married?" Officer 1 asked.

"Twenty-one years. Are you guys married?"

They shook their heads.

"Let me tell you, relationships take a lot of work. If you neglect them, you're heading to Splitsville." Then the words spilled out in a torrent. I ended up revealing a lot of embarrassing details, including my sex life with Peter. "So, you know how that works. I didn't want to have sex because I didn't feel emotionally close, and he didn't feel close without sex."

They just stood there, nodding their heads now and then and shifting on their feet.

"But now," I said, "I'm postmenopausal, and my libido is close to zero." I made a zero with my thumb and index finger.

They both glanced elsewhere.

"And on top of all that, we had to deal with the insane college admission process. Yeesh, that was so distressing."

Officer 1 interjected and asked if I'd prefer talking to counselors. I took that as a hint he'd rather be somewhere else.

"Right now?" I looked at the clock on the wall. It was 1:00 a.m.

The officer nodded.

"Is it free?" I asked.

"Yes, it is."

I hesitated, worried I might be wasting another precious resource, but snapped right out of it and said, "Sure, that'll be helpful."

While waiting for the counselors to arrive, I put Amber in her kennel and went back to bed to rest. The whole day had been bewildering, though I felt a twinge of guilt for dragging the two policemen into my whirlwind.

A half hour later, a pair of counselors arrived. I felt awkward and sheepish. The "truth serum" had started to wear off, replaced by my Japanese apologetic politeness. "Sorry for troubling you to come here this late," I said.

"No worries," the female counselor said. She handed me a business card that read, "Crisis Clinic: Immediate Help for People in Crisis. 24-Hour Crisis Line."

I was still drugged enough that I failed to register their names. Maybe Mary and Bob? Mary, probably in her fifties, was of medium build, and Bob, who looked to be in his sixties, was heavyset. Both of them wore glasses.

I invited them to sit in the dark living room, lit only by the kitchen lights two rooms away. It matched my somber mood. Also, I didn't want them to see my face clearly; I felt embarrassed and a bit ashamed of my neediness. I waved limply toward the kitchen and offered to serve them tea, but then sank down into the overstuffed armchair before they had a chance to answer.

Bob sat on the sofa adjacent to me and looked around, seemingly impressed by the spacious room with its high ceiling. Looking at the grand piano, he asked, "Who plays?"

"Oh, my son." I stared at the piano. "He's away at college in New York. No one plays now."

"So, would you walk us through what happened?" Mary asked.

I filled them in with a quick summary, including the guy named Holland America.

Bob raised an eyebrow. "That's a cruise line."

"What?" I was totally baffled but pretended it was no big deal. "I'm really impressed that they not only work around the clock but also provide a suicide prevention hotline."

They both laughed.

"Did you have any detailed plan for how to take your life?" Bob asked.

"Oh no, not really." I looked down. I'd involved so many people in what had just been a fleeting thought of suicide. "If I were serious, I'd google best methods, but I only vaguely imagined what it might be like to cut my wrists. But then I thought that would hurt. *A lot*. And be really messy."

"You didn't think of taking sleeping pills?" Bob asked.

For a moment I considered how easy it would be. How nice to drift off into peaceful sleep to the next world with no more agony or sorrow. "No." I shook my head. "Although that sounds like the most obvious and easiest way to go."

Bob and Mary exchanged a concerned look.

I could have easily turned their generous time and undivided attention into another talk therapy session by repeating my same self-pitying story—how easily my childhood wounds became reactivated when things got tough with my family. But it was late, and I was too tired.

Well, okay. I told Bob and Mary some of the story because I remember Bob saying, "Your husband sounds like he's emotionally stunted."

"For sure. He's a lot like his late father, who was extremely stoic and unemotional, even by Midwestern standards. But I think his steadiness helped to anchor and stabilize me more often than not."

I flashed back to the glorious day I gave birth to our son and to the image of Peter's glowing face as he thanked me repeatedly after the difficult delivery. How much he was willing to help out and support me during the most challenging initial period. Back then I had the illusion that together we could overcome anything.

Now, I wondered how our vulnerable marriage could have possibly dodged a direct hit. How had I thought all our problems, both old and new, would magically disappear as soon as David left for college? I must have been blind. I couldn't change anything in my life unless I changed myself.

Bob and Mary looked at me expectantly, as if waiting for me to say something more.

I pivoted to another topic. "I heard on NPR that in the past twenty years, the divorce rate has doubled for couples over fifty—the "gray divorce revolution," researchers are calling it. And I guess empty nesters are particularly vulnerable." I picked at a hangnail on my thumb.

"In my opinion, people have lost sight of what's truly important in life—like happily married parents and happy kids—while buying into the societal game of elitism, turning childrearing into too much of an enterprise, overinvesting in our children, and putting our marriages on the back burner," I added.

Biting the hangnail, I said pensively, "We both contributed to our conflicts, but I'd say I was about 70 percent guilty—maybe even 100 percent in some areas, like refusing sex, or at least never initiating it, or trivializing his sexual desire." I told them I'd become complacent and lazy, even delusional, to think that for us to survive all these years had been a testimony to our enduring marriage.

I was still in shock. We'd managed to survive Peter's medical school, a move across the country, a difficult childbirth, and early motherhood challenges with no support network, just as he began his brutal, five-year residency, in addition to our clueless parenting becoming a source of frequent bickering. If we made it through all that, couldn't we survive the empty nest, too, especially given how well our son turned out?

I rambled some more but caught myself before launching into a long, cultural discussion about how Japanese couples basically give up sex once their children are born, even though sex remains very important to American couples.

"And you know, I suck at multitasking," I said, apropos of nothing I'd said out loud. I told them I could attend to only one fire at a time, especially when my son's hormone-fueled teenage years coincided with my menopausal emotional roller coaster. And I was so preoccupied with putting out that fire, I became totally oblivious to the fact that our entire house was burning down.

When I looked up, it was 3:30 a.m. We'd been talking for two hours.

I thanked them for their home visit and escorted them to the front door. We shook hands, and I watched them walk down the front path, hoping they wouldn't stumble over the poorly lit step. The chilly autumn air blew in, and I pulled my robe across my chest and shut the door. Once again, the house became still.

I sipped a glass of water before returning to bed. As I lay down, I tried ignoring the empty space next to me and took several deep breaths to release the tension in my body. My rambling must have had a cathartic effect. I felt strangely comforted and uplifted, and I forgot all about the desperation that had permeated my day. I was also deeply touched and grateful to the caring individuals who had come to my rescue in the dead of night. By their compassion and kindness, they showed me that I was still worth saving, even when I had my doubts.

While trying to fall asleep, I felt a subtle but clear shift happen inside me, reawakening my gutsy self. As my tension began to ease, the voice in my head sounded more like a motivational coach than my usual vicious inner critic.

"You've overcome many obstacles and come so far from where you began," it said to me. "Even though the situation seems dire now, you can get through this, no matter the outcome." That was when I remembered the fish dream I'd had after moving to America. I was the fish released into the water. I had thrived then. If I didn't give up, I could be like that fish again and grow stronger.

Second Honeymoon

July, 2017

I believe there must have been some divine intervention that enabled me to transform such a desperate situation into a hopeful one. How lucky I was that what Peter wanted from me was almost exactly what I wanted for myself—to be happy, content, and fulfilled, regaining self-confidence and being more positive—reviving the person I used to be, the person he'd married. It wasn't easy. I'd almost completely forgotten how to be happy, but I made subtle positive changes each day, beginning with self-care and focusing on what would bring me joy.

As we tried to repair our marriage, Peter insisted I go back to work and suggested a preschool, which I thought was a great idea since I missed working with little children. Peter and I went on dates, which we'd seldom done before our nest had become empty, dining out and going to movies, even to *Beautiful: The Carole King Musical*. We also took dance lessons and participated in a workshop for couples to learn how to communicate and connect at a deep emotional level.

As I regained my strength and confidence, I no longer fixated on the future outcome with Peter. More importantly, I learned how to relax and be in the moment and really enjoyed myself. My newfound zest for life unleashed the sense of being alive and in love with Peter again more than any other time I could remember. These were the keys to regaining my happy self, which I realized had always been there. They'd just needed a shock to shake them free. With growing faith in myself, I believed that even if things didn't work out with Peter, I would be okay and in a much better place to start over on my own.

Throughout this marital separation, David remained supportive of me and didn't seem concerned about our marriage. Perhaps he was too consumed by acclimating to college life, or maybe he sensed that because I seemed to be happy and doing well, he could focus on himself.

Missing Peter so much brought out my untapped potential for passion. We had a lot to catch up on after our lost decade or more. Our empty nest transformed into a love nest, which felt like a second honeymoon. It was a good sign that he still found me attractive after all of these years.

It might sound out of character for my otherwise stoic and humble Midwestern husband, but in bed Peter transformed into an amorous lover with bottomless passion. As for me, not so much. My style was more cut-to-the-chase and get-down-to-business. Although sex hadn't been my thing for many years, I was definitely willing to accommodate. I went to see my primary care doctor for my recurring UTIs, for which she prescribed a low-dose antibiotic to take before and after intercourse.

When I requested a larger quantity, she widened her eyes. "How many times a week do you have sex?"

"Umm, three to four maybe. Sometimes twice a day," I said with a grin.

The major breakthrough came when I realized Peter was actually a kind, warmhearted, and empathetic person who wanted me to be happy, not the selfish, demanding, and unfeeling person I'd made him out to be over the years of squabbling. I began to accept that my rejection of him had caused him to shut down emotionally and become distant. As we cultivated the ability to discuss sensitive issues without getting defensive, I understood how it had pained him to see me depressed for so long and not be able to make any difference. One of the important ways he felt close to me was through sexual bonding, but he couldn't have that, either, as my mind was often wandering elsewhere. I had no idea how closely sex was tied in with his sense of self and identity and that he'd felt rejected and hurt by me over and over again. This had caused him to build walls around his heart and stop expecting anything, which eventually led him to conclude there was no point in us both staying in an unhappy marriage.

I heard him clearly. I wish we hadn't needed to go through all this in order to change our perspectives, but lucky for us, being separated and on the brink of divorce served as a catalyst for more open and constructive communication that, in the end, helped us foster a positive relationship.

Not that everything went smoothly. It took time and effort to heal our festering resentment, but after nine months of separation, I had regained Peter's trust, and he decided to move back in. It felt like a miracle. I was immensely grateful for his willingness to give us another chance and start our new chapter together. Surprisingly (or maybe not), as a byproduct of shifting to a more positive attitude and mindset, my chronic pain lessened dramatically, and I rarely needed to take Aleve anymore. I experienced firsthand the mind-body link and the power of positive thinking to heal physical and emotional ailments. My repressed toxic emotions had been wreaking havoc on my body. All the massages and alternative therapies in the world wouldn't help if I continued to beat myself up with negative self-talk.

One month after Peter moved back in, I renounced my Japanese citizenship and became a US citizen—finally, after living in the United States for thirty-four years. It was largely a symbolic gesture to free myself from the past, especially from my old, wounded Japanese self.

My mother is still alive, and her health has been relatively stable. While setting healthy boundaries with her, I've been checking in with weekly calls and sending her a monthly allowance. We still have differences of opinion and perspective, and our chats are usually brief, but our relationship is friendly. It's much easier these days to forgive and accept her for who she is as I've become more understanding of her limitations. I've also come to terms with my own past by accepting—and even appreciating—my younger self for getting me through challenging times.

As I reflect on my journey, I realize our past lives inside us, no matter how much we want to deny it or try to run from it. No matter how firmly we decide not to become our parents, we still carry some of their imprints and risk passing on trauma to our children. Becoming conscious of the cycle of intergenerational trauma can, therefore, lead to taking active steps to address and break it. This awareness was crucial, not only in helping to heal from my own childhood trauma, but also in creating a better future for my child.

Despite many ups and downs over the years, my deep inner journey of self-reflection cultivated greater self-acceptance by uncovering the root causes of my lifelong struggles. I feel extremely grateful and fortunate that I was also able to rebuild secure relationships with my husband and son.

Like the fish in my fish dream, I embarked on my lone journey in 1983, leaving my dysfunctional family in Japan to pursue a better life, home, and family in America. I have found a place in Seattle I can call home, where I live with my own loving family and have a beautiful garden that attracts wild animal visitors. Tending to hummingbirds in my backyard garden, watching mason bees go in and out of their nesting tubes, playing with bumblebees, hand-feeding wild bunnies—these seemingly ordinary moments bring me joy each day. Even without a pond, this place is my sanctuary grounded in nature, where I find happiness in simply being myself.

I'm at peace with my past and my present. With a renewed sense of self, I look forward to the future while continuing to practice being in the moment.

Acknowledgments

I would like to express my heartfelt gratitude to the many wonderful people who were integral to my writing journey and contributed to the successful completion of this book.

First and foremost, I extend my profound appreciation to Dr. Barbara Turner-Vesselago, who taught me how to write from "the larger Self" and develop self-trust in the writing process. Without her influential mentorship in my early stages of writing, I wouldn't have written a single word and might never have discovered my passion for storytelling.

Thanks also to Kelly Malone, Suzanne Morrison, and Theo Nestor, whose fantastic coaching, guidance, and encouragement have been instrumental in my growth as a writer and in sculpting my initial work.

Further gratitude to:

Gail Folkins and Sarah Williams, for their narrative assessments and insightful critiques, which greatly enhanced my early drafts.

Claire Dederer at Hugo House and Debra Gwartney, Scott Korb, and Mike Magnuson at Pacific University Oregon—gifted and inspiring teachers who gave me their unparalleled instruction and advice.

The exceptionally talented editors Michelle Barker, Justine Chan, and Lorraine Fico-White, for their outstanding assistance in sharpening and polishing my work into its final form.

Rose Friel, Caitlin Hamilton Summie, Libby Jordan, and Peggy Holsclaw, for their invaluable assistance and support.

My dear writer friends—especially Ting Ting Cheng, Claire Cuccio, Imara, Leslie Johansen Nack, Sophia Kouidou-Giles, Linda Lockwood, Vicki Pinkerton, Dorothy Rice, Soula Stefanopoulos, Dr. Fletch Taylor, Joyce Tomlinson, and Vicki Pinkerton—for their constructive feedback and camaraderie.

Brooke Warner, Krissa Lagos, Julie Metz, Megan Milton, and the incredibly welcoming and supportive She Writes community, for their mutual respect and bonds of sisterhood.

My lifelong friend Dr. John Wallace and my Napa host family, for their love and unwavering support over the decades.

I am also deeply grateful to Drs. Boadie Dunlop and Stephen Murphy-Shigematsu, Janine Brodine, Anne Liu Kellor, and Lori Matsukawa, for their generosity in reading my work. Your kind words of endorsement mean so much to me.

Finally, I want to thank my loving husband and son for being my anchors for all these years. Their enduring support and faith in me have carried me through the most challenging times, and I am forever grateful to have them by my side on this journey.

About the Author

Shigeko Ito grew up in Japan and immigrated to the United States in her twenties to pursue higher education. She studied early childhood development and education, earning a PhD in Education from Stanford University. Drawing on cross-cultural experiences and academic expertise, she explores themes of trauma, resilience, and healing, with a particular focus on childhood emotional neglect. Her writing has appeared on the Complex Post-Traumatic Stress Disorder (CPTSD) Foundation blog and the Anxiety and Depression Association of America (ADAA) website. She worked for many years at a Montessori preschool and is an avid animal lover, especially of dogs, who enjoys birding, gardening, and raising mason bees. She lives in Seattle, Washington, with her husband of thirty years.